General Editor: Robin Gilmour

Doris Lessing

JEANNETTE KING

Tutor in Literature for the Open University

Edward Arnold

A division of Hodder & Stoughton

LONDON   NEW YORK   MELBOURNE   AUCKLAND

First published in Great Britain 1989

Distributed in the USA by Routledge, Chapman and Hall, Inc.
29 West 35th Street, New York, NY 10001

British Library Cataloguing in Publication Data

King, Jeanette
    Doris Lessing. — (Modern fiction).
    1. Fiction in English. Lessing, Doris, 1919–
    critical studies
    I. Title   II. Series
    823'.914

    ISBN 0–7131–6555–3

Typeset in 10/12 pt Sabon Compugraphic
by Colset Private Limited, Singapore
Printed and bound in Great Britain for Edward Arnold, the
educational, academic and medical publishing division of Hodder
and Stoughton Limited, 41 Bedford Square, London WC1B 3DQ by
Biddles Ltd, Guildford and King's Lynn

Contents

To Jon

General Editor's Preface

Fiction constitutes the largest single category of books published each year, and the discussion of fiction is at the heart of the present revolution in literary theory, yet the reader looking for substantial guidance to some of the most interesting prose writers of the twentieth century – especially those who have written in the past 30 or 40 years – is often poorly served. Specialist studies abound, but up-to-date maps of the field are harder to come by. *Modern Fiction* has been designed to supply that lack. It is a new series of authoritative introductory studies of the chief writers and movements in the history of twentieth-century fiction in English. Each volume has been written by an expert in the field and offers a fresh and accessible reading of the writer's work in the light of the best recent scholarship and criticism. Biographical information is provided, consideration of the writer's relationship to the world of their times, and detailed readings of selected texts. The series includes short-story writers as well as novelists, contemporaries as well as the classic moderns and their successors, Commonwealth writers as well as British and American; and there are volumes on themes and groups as well as on individual figures. At a time when twentieth-century fiction is increasingly studied and talked about, *Modern Fiction* provides short, helpful, stimulating introductions designed to encourage fresh thought and further enquiry.

Robin Gilmour

Preface

In April 1988, Thames Television devoted a complete edition of *The South Bank Show* to Doris Lessing, introducing her as one of the world's most important living novelists. What has earned her such a reputation? Her earliest novels and stories, published in the 1950s, were greeted as fiction of 'commitment', so that she was linked with a number of influential radical writers, including the 'Angry Young Men'. Lessing's writing on Africa in particular was regarded as an important contribution to their critique of colonialism and the sterile political and cultural life of post-war Britain. The novels she wrote in the 1960s were heralded as valuable contributions to causes as varied as the growing Women's Movement, the Campaign for Nuclear Disarmament, and the Anti-Psychiatry movement of R.D. Laing. Throughout her career, her work has consistently engaged with issues of critical concern to the modern world, and with philosophies ranging from Marxism to Sufism. In the process, it has become increasingly critical of Western European culture, and of the rational, liberal humanist tradition so central to it.

But Lessing's reputation does not rest solely on the issues with which her novels deal, important though they may be. Her significance as a modern novelist derives also from her adventurousness, her readiness to experiment with the novel form, even at the risk of losing readers devoted to her earlier realist fiction. Refusing to be categorized according to either theme or form, Doris Lessing has continued to develop as a novelist, exploring issues both personal and political through whichever form has appeared to her most appropriate.

Her early novels belong to the tradition of European realism, of critical realism, but even here there is a sense of strain and dissatisfaction with a form which many see as embodying those very ideologies from which she is attempting to distance herself. The aim of this study is to demonstrate, by close discussion of those novels which mark significant stages in her development, the variety of formal experiments Doris Lessing has undertaken. I also hope to demonstrate that those experiments were a necessary and inevitable consequence of her search for literary forms which would allow for a more radical critique of Western culture.

I shall be reading the novels along lines developed by Jacques Lacan, a French psychoanalyst, whose analysis of the individual's acquisition of identity through language has provided me with an approach to Lessing's novels which I have found consistently relevant. I will also be arguing that Lessing's analysis is implicitly feminist, in the sense that, like many recent radical feminists, it challenges the 'humanity' of a culture which ascribes value to what has been traditionally defined as 'male', and remains male-dominated in so many of its central assumptions and power-structures.

It has been suggested that women's literature is the literature of the colonized: that women write from the position of a sub-culture upon which have been imposed the values and structures of the dominant patriarchal culture. If this is so, then the novels of a woman brought up in Southern Rhodesia could be said to be doubly colonized. Doris Lessing writes from the point of view of someone who is part of the tradition of Western European literature, and yet distanced from it, writing from its margins. This 'marginal' perspective is one of her greatest strengths as a writer, giving her a freedom to explore and analyse the 'centres' of our culture which she has fully and imaginatively exploited.

I would like to thank Robin Gilmour for his careful reading of my manuscript and for his constructive comments on it.

Jeannette King
Aberdeen 1988

A Note on Editions

Quotations from Doris Lessing's novels are taken from the editions listed below, and will be identified by page numbers (in brackets) after each quotation. Paperback editions have been used wherever possible.

The Grass is Singing	Grafton Books,	1980
Children of Violence sequence	Panther Books	
Martha Quest		1966
The Four-Gated City		1972
The Golden Notebook	Panther Books	1973
Briefing for a Descent into Hell	Panther Books	1972
Canopus in Argos sequence	Granada	
Shikasta		1981
The Making of the Representative for Planet 8		1983
The Sentimental Agents in the Volyen Empire		1985
The Good Terrorist	Grafton Books	1986

1

The Grass is Singing

(i) Doris Lessing and the Realist Tradition

Doris Lessing published her first novel, *The Grass is Singing*, in 1950, a year after her arrival in England. But the novel had been written in Southern Rhodesia, so that one would not expect her view of colonial life to provide much evidence of that marginal stance which I have suggested characterizes her work. However, her analysis of Southern Rhodesian society or – as she herself puts it – 'white people anywhere south of the Zambezi',[1] is also a critique of the European outlook, in particular that of the British, which gave birth to the colony. The novel therefore reveals the contradictions inherent in the colonial experience and its ambiguous relationship to the 'centre' of Empire.

Early reviews of *The Grass is Singing* were quick to relate the novel to the tradition of European fiction,[2] to the classics which Lessing had read during her isolated childhood on a Rhodesian farm. But a more relevant influence for her purposes was that of Olive Schreiner, whose novel *The Story of an African Farm* (1883) she describes as the first 'real' book she had read with Africa for a setting: 'Here was the substance of truth, and not from England or Russia or France or America, necessitating all kinds of mental translations, switches, correspon-

---

1. 'Interview with Doris Lessing by Roy Newquist' in Paul Schlueter, ed., *A Small Personal Voice: Doris Lessing: Essays, Reviews, Interviews* (New York: Vintage Books, 1975), p. 46.
2. See Selma Burkom, *Doris Lessing: A Checklist of Primary and Secondary Sources* (New York: Whitson Publishers, 1973) for a list of reviews of the early fiction.

dences, but reflecting what I knew and could see'.[3] Its relevance was that it demonstrated the possibility of adapting the traditions of European fiction to the African experience. Doris Lessing's first extended statement on the function of the novel, written in 1957, confirms the importance of these early influences: 'For me the highest point of literature was the novel of the nineteenth century, the work of Tolstoy, Stendhal, Dostoevsky, Balzac, Turgenev, Chekhov; the work of the great realists'.[4]

Given the extensive debate that has taken place in recent years over the nature and function of 'Realism', we need at this stage to establish its meaning for Doris Lessing. In praising Schreiner's novel for 'reflecting' Africa as she knew it, she appears to invoke a simple 'reflection' theory of literature which records what is already there. Critical of the parochialism of so many British writers of the period, whose 'horizons are bounded by their immediate experience of British life and standards',[5] she appears to see her own writing as a means of broadening her readers' horizons. Like many of those nineteenth-century writers she admires, she will draw her reader's attention to social and political evils of which they are ignorant. Critics of her early work clearly saw her 'realism' in just such terms, often treating it rather dismissively as 'thoroughly competent *reporting* of social evils of all kinds which comes near to journalism' (my italics).[6] The many points of resemblance between Doris Lessing's fiction and non-fiction further encourage such a reading.[7]

But what Lessing primarily looks for at this time from the great classical realists is commitment to humanity, a commitment that only comes from their understanding of their own world:

> Once a writer has a feeling of responsibility, as a human being, for the other human beings he influences, it seems to me he must become a humanist, and must feel himself as an instrument of change for good or for bad . . . he must see himself, to use the socialist phrase, as an architect of the soul . . . But if one is going to be an architect, one must have a vision to build towards, and that vision must spring from the nature of the world we live in.[8]

3. Lessing, 'Afterword to *The Story of an African Farm* by Olive Schreiner' in *Small Personal Voice*, p. 99.
4. 'The Small Personal Voice', *Op. cit.* p. 4.
5. *Op. cit.*, p. 15.
6. 'Local Colour', *The Times*, 11 July 1953, p. 8.
7. See 'My Father', *Small Personal Voice*, and *Going Home* (revised edition, London: Panther Books, 1968).
8. *Small Personal Voice*, pp. 6–7.

Doris Lessing here appears to be articulating a more sophisticated form of reflection theory such as is found in the work of the Marxist critic, Georg Lukacs. Her work at this period could be described as what he calls 'critical realism', as opposed to realism of surface, or verisimilitude.[9] Such writing provides not a mirror-view of reality, but knowledge of it: it makes sense of historical processes by revealing the relationship between the human subject and the objective world, thus embodying knowledge of the structures of reality. This view is formulated in slightly different terms by Raymond Williams, in 'Realism and the Contemporary Novel' which was published around the same time as Lessing's essay, and shows similar preoccupations. He defines the 'typical', which is a central feature of this kind of realism, as 'the most deeply characteristic human experience, in an individual or in a society'. Williams goes on to say of realist fiction:

> society is not a background against which the personal relationships are studied, nor are the individuals merely illustrations of aspects of the way of life. Every aspect of personal life is radically affected by the quality of the general life, yet the general life is seen at its most important in completely personal terms . . . In the highest realism, society is seen in fundamentally personal terms, and persons, through relationships, in fundamentally social terms.[10]

The relevance of such an analysis to Doris Lessing's early work can be demonstrated by examining the first chapter of *The Grass is Singing*. The newspaper report of the 'Murder Mystery' with which it begins seems to place it within a documentary, journalistic tradition. But this opening merely makes use of a representational convention which disguises the fictional nature of the work, creating the illusion of 'reality'. Lessing believes that, unlike the journalist, 'collecting facts and information', the novelist 'has to go inwards to probe out the truth'.[11] To this end, as well as getting the surface details right, she uses metaphor to suggest the implications and effects of the social structures under analysis. For her realism is an art which 'springs so vigorously and naturally from a strongly-held, though not necessarily intellectually-defined, view of life that it absorbs symbolism'.[12] Her evocation of life on an African farm conveys the physical harshness of such an existence,

9. *The Meaning of Contemporary Realism*, trans. J. and N. Mander (London: Merlin Press, 1963).
10. *The Long Revolution* (Harmondsworth: Penguin Books, 1965), pp. 304–5, and p. 314.
11. *Going Home*, p. 63.
12. *Small Personal Voice*, p. 4.

for poor whites as well as for blacks. The dryness, dust and oppressive heat induce in the heroine, Mary Turner, feelings of exhaustion and apathy, but they also function as signifiers of sterility and emotional aridity with much the same force as in T.S. Eliot's *Waste Land*, quoted as an epigraph to the novel. The oppressiveness of these elements further signifies to Mary the feeling of being acted upon by an inescapable fate, forced to re-enact her mother's unhappy, poverty-stricken existence. To the reader it may suggest the oppressiveness of the whole system and the stifling weight of ideology which underpins it. Similarly the store is explicitly identified by the narrator as a symbol of Southern African society (p. 32) as an exploitative economic structure. But for Mary it also has a personal dimension, embodying the childhood from which she cannot escape, and at her death housing her murderer. Through symbolism the text operates at both the personal and political level, ultimately demonstrating the identity of the two, according to the best traditions of nineteenth-century realism.

Many recent critics have, however, suggested that realist fiction tends to encourage, through its frequent use of an omniscient narrator, 'closed' readings, which they identify as a major weakness of the form.[13] This novel instead invites an awareness of its capacity to 'mean' many things through a narrative method which prevents such closure. The third-person narrator's understanding of the events narrated is limited and variable. The narrative voice – who speaks – remains constant, the voice of an unspecified, impersonal narrator. But the 'mood' or point of view – who sees – changes.[14] The opening newspaper report is typical of external focalization – adopting a point of view external to the object of study – delivered by an observer whose lack of inside knowledge of the murderer Moses engenders the first 'murder mystery' – not 'whodunnit', but 'why?'. But the generalizations and assertions which follow are confident conjectures as to what 'must have been'. These are the inevitable conclusions of the insider, based on a body of shared experience and unspoken assumptions which make all human behaviour predictable. The text of *The Grass is Singing* thus draws attention to the partiality of this narrative voice.

This element of bias becomes clearer with the use of free indirect speech, where the narrative's internal focalization – observing character and event from within the consciousness of a specific individual – becomes more obvious.

> It was not right to seclude themselves like that; it was a slap in the face of everyone else; what had they got to be so stuck-up about? What, indeed! Living the way they did! That little box of a house – it was forgivable as a temporary dwelling, but not to live in permanently. Why, some natives (though not many, thank heavens) had houses as good; and it would give them a bad impression to see white people living in such a way. (p. 10)

This passage employs the tone and language appropriate to the attitudes expressed, so that the third-person narrative (using the same 'voice'), is now coloured by the thoughts and feelings of a particular kind of person – the successful white settler. The narrative voice speaks from outside the African experience, but from within that of the white community.

But if this inside view is shown to be biased, the point of view of the judgmental outsider is also called into question through the novel's presentation of its most obvious representative, Tony Marston. This young Britisher, newly arrived in the colony, takes over the management of the Turners' farm when their mutual breakdown makes their departure essential. Marston articulates those questions and criticisms which we would expect of an outsider, thus acting as a focal point for the European reader. However, his feeling that he ought to speak in Moses's defence, to explain the background to the case, collapses in the face of the unwillingness of the police to recognize anything other than the facts. He is easily silenced. His idealism, his 'progressive' beliefs about race, are exposed as superficial abstractions, fading when tested by social pressure and self-interest. Quick to diagnose the hypocrisy of Rhodesian society, he is blind to his own. His complacency as well as his criticisms are thus offered for evaluation. Through him, the novel both articulates and undermines the authority of the liberal outsider, particularly that of the British, more explicitly condemned in Doris Lessing's non-fiction.[15] Marston, therefore, performs an important function in indicating how the novel is to be read. He senses that 'the important thing, the thing that really mattered . . . was to understand the background, the circumstances, the characters of Dick and Mary, the pattern of their lives' (p. 23). In pointing to the need to understand the deep-rooted causes of Mary's murder, he draws attention to the need to understand the different points of view, though not necessarily to exonerate them.

15. See e.g. *Going Home*, p. 64 and pp. 302–3.

Therefore, while Marston's emphasis is primarily on vindicating the murderer, the novel functions also as a kind of vindication of the woman who 'got herself murdered', whose death won not the sympathy of her white neighbours, but their hatred. The retrospective narrative which follows Chapter 1 has a more specific internal focalization: events are consistently seen from Mary's point of view, apart from a brief excursion into Dick's. As always with this kind of subjectively oriented narrative, the problem of reliability arises, exacerbated in this case by the evidence of Mary's gradual mental breakdown. In the absence of a clear authorial point of view, privileged over that of the characters, we nevertheless have to accept this dominant point of view as it stands, attempting to evaluate and make sense of its perceptions as best we can.

If there is one point of view which we might expect to have particular claims on the reader's sympathy, to be privileged by the author, it is surely that of Moses himself. Yet here the narrative is curiously silent. Moses's inner life remains largely inaccessible, since this character is consistently seen from the point of view of an observer, from his very first appearance after the murder with the words, 'Here I am.' He is described: 'a great powerful man, black as polished linoleum' (p. 16). But whereas it is conventional in realist fiction for external appearance to be a key to the inner life, no clues are provided here – his face remains 'expressionless, indifferent', as 'blank' as when Mary first saw him. There is surely a suggestion here that white readers – of character or of fiction – are not capable of interpreting black experience. The white farmers are content with a stereotypical interpretation of his motives for murder – what is every black servant but a potential thief? There is some attempt to penetrate Moses's thinking through Mary's eyes during their brief relationship. Her attempt to read his face is an indication that the black/white, servant/mistress barrier has been breached and that she is forced to recognize his individuality. But the victim is not alive to bear witness to the motives for the murder. The reader is told that this is his 'moment of triumph' (p. 219), but the precise nature of this triumph remains problematic, as do his feelings towards the victim. The observer can only note Moses's apparent indifference. The limits of realism are here drawn by the apparent impossibility of imaginative entry into attitudes and values shaped by such alien experience: like Marston, no white person, it seems, could 'even begin to imagine the mind of a native' (p. 29).[16] The narrative

16. See also *Going Home*, p. 65.

method thus enacts the distance between Europe and Africa which is inherent in the colonial situation.

Nineteenth-century European Realism thus embodied a literary tradition and the kind of social commitment with which, in the 1950s, Doris Lessing could identify. However, she rejected the implicit assurance and authority of the omniscient narrator so often associated with that tradition. She adopts instead a narrative method which works against any final, closed reading, any authoritative sanctioning of a single attitude as 'correct'. She introduces a degree of questioning, of uncertainty, which indicates her awareness of the formal and cultural contradictions inherent in such an identification. The colonial experience presented in *The Grass is Singing* is itself contradictory – the colonialist is by origin an outsider, imposing his (usually) will on what he sees as an undeveloped people and country; he is equally assertive, when defending this position, that only insiders like himself can judge the system he has created. An outsider in his adopted country, he also exists on the margins of 'Home', Britain. Unable or unwilling to assimilate and comprehend the experience of the Africa he has colonized, he is equally unable to accept the attitudes of the British who observe from the privileged position of the centre of Empire. For a woman, the position is even more complex, since she also exists on the margins of 'her' own society. I now want to consider the means by which the novel demonstrates the ideological processes which determine 'centre' and 'margin'.

(ii) The Ideological Process

I have suggested that *The Grass is Singing* resists any 'closed reading', any attempt to impose a single, authoritative meaning. Instead it offers a variety of ways of understanding what lies beneath the 'facts' of the murder. While it is tempting to see the novel as primarily about the colour bar, Doris Lessing has repeatedly asserted that there is more at issue than this: 'if one has been at great pains to choose a theme which is more general, people are so struck by the enormity and ugliness of the colour prejudices which must be shown in it that what one has tried to say gets lost.'[17] What then is her more general theme? Through each of the readings that follow I hope to demonstrate a preoccupation with ideology – the system of values and beliefs by which individuals represent their relationship to material reality, and

17. *Op. cit.*, p. 18.

which, once dominant, are used to justify existing political and social systems.

So to those readers who wish to understand life in Southern Africa, Doris Lessing recommends novels like *Anna Karenina*, on the grounds that they illustrate economic divisions similar to those separating black from white. Adopting a Marxist approach, she argues that 'colour-feeling is basically money-feeling . . . in spite of all the rationales of racialism . . . The white man would strike if they were paid the same, while they still worked together.'[18] *The Grass is Singing* gives prominence to these economic factors in the deterministic presentation both of the poor whites, Dick and Mary, and of those who are more successful. Mary's hostility to men and her loathing of the African bush can be attributed to a childhood impoverished by her father's drinking and embittered by her mother's struggles for economic survival. Dick's failures in farming can similarly be related to an economic system which favours those like Charlie Slatter, who exploit the land and the natives, rather than the more conservation-minded Dick.

Economic factors alone, however, do not account for the loss of self-esteem and social approval experienced by the Turners. In this society, financial success is a guarantee of racial superiority. Without it, the white man or woman is reduced to the level of the native. The individual's failure thus threatens the myth of white superiority, according to which black men are poor because they lack the ability and willingness to work which have made the white man rich. It is not Christian charity which impels Charlie to help out the Turners but ideology – the need to preserve the myth. Nor do economic factors fully explain Moses's motives, and his feeling of triumph over Dick. If the economic degradation which is depicted so vividly were sufficient motive, then why not kill Dick himself, the paymaster? The answer involves the personal relationship between Moses and Mary, and their perception of its interaction with these wider economic and social realities – again the issue is one of ideology.

A feminist reading might help to explain further the operation of these economic and social forces on Mary. To what extent is she presented as the victim of pressure to conform to a female stereotype? She initially resists the traditional role of wife by refusing adulthood, remaining 'girlish', and only finally marrying in reaction to gossip about her single state. She continues to evade the physical dimensions of marriage, submitting to sex without giving herself, and adopting a pseudo-maternal attitude to Dick to avoid confronting him as woman to man. Pregnancy itself is totally repellent to her.

Mary only experiences real satisfaction on the farm when she is forced – through Dick's illness – to play a masculine role. She exploits to the full the sense of power this situation gives her: she is a 'virago', whose adherence to the 'rules' makes the already appalling conditions of work so unbearable that many of the natives leave. She is also a more efficient farm manager than Dick, having a far keener eye for the best ways of maximizing profit. She is not however allowed to assume the role of the white boss, since she – as a woman – exists on the margins of the black/white power structure. Her energy and efficiency threaten Dick's position in this structure – he needs 'masculine talk', even with Charlie whom he dislikes, to restore his self-assurance with his wife. Her attempt to usurp male authority is indeed seized on as the popular explanation for her murder – being a woman, she did not know how to handle natives properly.

Denied this 'masculine' role, and unable to conform to the acceptable roles of wife and mother, Mary lapses once more into passivity, taking on 'the voice of the suffering female' (p. 83), which she had watched her mother enact for so many years. Her mental and physical breakdown can thus be seen as the result of the limitations imposed on this once independent and active woman, who ironically married to be her *own* mistress.

But while such a reading brings out the role of gender in Mary's tragedy, it fails to take into account the complexity with which she is presented. Nor does it account for her relationship with Moses, other than – rather simplistically – as an outlet for the frustrations of a bored housewife. Above all, it fails to take into account Mary's complicity with this repressive patriarchal society. As if to underline this, the narrator takes Mary to task for an 'arid feminism', grounded in envy of men's 'easy' lives, asserting that, as a privileged single white woman, Mary is 'free' enough to have become 'a person on her own account' (p. 38). This rare intrusion of a direct judgement on the narrator's part inevitably appears to carry the weight of authorial judgement. And Mary's behaviour at this time is used to validate such a judgement. Living in an institution as similar to her beloved boarding school as possible, she is totally dependent on others both domestically, and socially, expecting to be entertained by men without forming any emotional attachments. She evades responsibility for her own life by marrying Dick. Mary is, in fact, not an essential inner self trapped within repressive social structures, as my first 'feminist' reading would suggest, but two selves – a conforming self and a rebellious self, each a social construct. It is not simply that her desires are frustrated by society, but that what she desires is itself the product of that society and therefore at odds with the needs of her rebellious self.[19]

Like all children, Mary learns to repress what is forbidden, or disapproved of by society – in particular forbidden sexual desires. What is repressed then enters, or rather forms, the unconscious, only manifesting itself in metaphoric substitutions for what cannot be admitted to consciousness. In her case, the repression of desire for her father is reinforced by her close identification with her mother and thus with her mother's conflict with her father. The choice between identification with the father or with the mother faces all infants, but is one which recent feminist criticism has identified as being acutely critical for the female child. For her, the choice is between identification with the mother, which renders her marginal to the symbolic order of language – a system in which the patriarchal order is inscribed – or raising herself to the symbolic stature of the father, deriving her identity and power from that order, and thus repressing those qualities labelled as 'female'.[20] Each choice involves the repression of the other self. It is thus not just the Oedipal desire for the father that is repressed, but that part of herself which identifies with the father – a more dominant angry self which she learns to identify as masculine and therefore unacceptable in her female self.

Mary's forbidden desire therefore transfers itself onto socially approved goals, onto the girlish role of the 'free', single woman, always 'fun', always available on every social occasion. The ideal self she pursues is a cultural ideal. But the pursuit of such an ideal inevitably creates a sense of inadequacy, of the gap between what one is and what one aspires to be. Thus when Mary overhears others talking about her apparent asexuality, a sense of lack is created, together with an awareness of the loss of social approval, which leads directly and tragically to her marriage. This incident also makes glaringly apparent the instability of so-called 'identity', the absence of an autonomous,

19. As I indicated in my Preface, I shall be drawing here and throughout this book on the theories of Jacques Lacan, a French psychoanalyst who has reinterpreted Freud in the light of post-structuralist theories of discourse. For a helpful introduction to his complex ideas, see Terry Eagleton, *Literary Theory: An Introduction* (Oxford: Basil Blackwell, 1983), pp. 163–74, or for a fuller discussion, Elizabeth Wright, *Psychoanalytic Criticism: Theory in Practice* (London: Methuen, 1984), pp. 107–22.
20. I am indebted here to Julia Kristeva's feminist re-reading of Freud. See Toril Moi, *Textual/Sexual Politics: Feminist Literary Theory* (London: Methuen, 1985), pp. 150–73.

unified essential self. Because 'her idea of herself was destroyed', she has to 'recreate herself', but, feeling completely 'hollow' and 'empty' inside, has only the 'distorted mirror' image of woman offered by the cinema screen to guide her (p. 45). This image, like that offered by her friends, is an image of incompleteness, of a woman needing a man, of the woman who ought to get married.

When Mary takes on the role of 'master', the repressed self that identifies with the father is brought into play, and at this point the interface between sexual and racial ideology becomes clear. For the repressed anger Mary feels towards Dick can be turned against the natives in a form which is legitimized as her anger against him is not. When she hits Moses with the sambok, the violence underlying this system is brought vividly into the open, all the more powerfully in contrast to Mary's habitual apathy. Mary is thus a far more successful embodiment than Dick of the white settler myth – a far shrewder exploiter of the land and the natives, so completely has she assumed the role and ideology of white supremacy. Nevertheless, Mary's act of violence against Moses also represents an illegitimate usurpation of male power, releasing feelings so frightening to Mary's conforming self that some way has to be found of countering this transgression. By a process of metaphoric substitution, the forbidden desire for the father becomes a desire for Moses, the trigger for the release of the forbidden violent emotions, so that the primal taboo on desire for the parent is safeguarded, though at the cost of transgressing the taboo on desire for the black.

But the transgression of racial ideology is in turn compensated for by a new conformity to sexual ideology. In her relationship with Moses Mary acts out the traditional female role in an almost parodic manner. With Moses her will (within patriarchal ideology a male prerogative) is suspended, and she returns to the status of the weeping child, helplessly dependent on the male, underlining the extent of the father/Moses substitution which has taken place. Mary yields her dominant position, submitting to Moses's 'almost fatherly' gentleness: 'she could hear his voice, firm and kind, like a father commanding her' (p. 161), and she surrenders responsibility for herself to him. Her desire for social approval has been displaced onto a figure which, in its girlish flirtatiousness, is a parody of that youthful self in which she last found general approval, but with the addition of that sexuality in which she was then found wanting. She has finally succeeded in becoming what she was thought to be incapable of, as is evident from her triumphant 'They said I was not like that' (p. 199).

Mary's relationship with Moses is, therefore, richly ambiguous. On the one hand it constitutes a regression, the triumph of the conforming female self, helplessly dependent on a father figure. On the other, it represents a challenge to racist ideology, indicating a potential liberation from ideology. Such a growth of awareness would have been impossible if Mary had remained alone in the city, inviolate. Her horror of human physicality, including her own, aroused so intensely by the sight of the native women suckling their babies in the open, has gradually changed into the kind of fascination she feels when she watches Moses washing. His overt resentment of this invasion of his privacy forces her to acknowledge his humanity, and acts as a challenge to her white authority. The physical thus leads into the personal, which is at once the political, since her relationship with Moses challenges ideology at so many levels. When Charlie visits the Turners, he is horrified not simply by Mary's flirtation with a native, but by the fact that she has gone native, wearing cloth sold for natives in the store.

While this emergent self – significantly named her 'darker' self – tries to shut out everything 'that would revive the code' (p. 199) of white settlerdom, the conforming self which is the product of ideology cannot acknowledge the existence of this repressed self, so that this splitting can only lead to fragmentation and mental breakdown. Ironically this breakdown represents a kind of 'triumph' of the unconscious self which has been 'colonized' by the rational self, just as Moses's murder of Mary is his 'triumph' over his white masters. Just before her death, she again hopes a young man will rescue her 'from herself' (p. 213) – not from Moses. At the end of her life she still sees herself as an uncomprehending victim, but is aware of another self judging and condemning her relationship with Moses. She is split into two selves, the one who feels totally without power, and the other whose power is 'borrowed' from the system which enforces her own oppression. In this sense the popular view that she 'got herself murdered' (p. 11) contains an element of truth.

The novel therefore forges a powerful link between the construction of individual identity and subjectivity through the repression of unacceptable desires, and the construction of a mythical racial identity through the repression of another race. Both black Africans and white women are perceived as children according to the patriarchal ideology of white Africa. The myth of white settlerdom rests on an image of the firm but just master, taking charge of an undeveloped country and the noble African child of nature who needs just such guidance. It is also a myth of male domination – of the strong hand needed to tame the wild. According to this ideology, Dick, with his boyish whistle, his love of the veld and his easy-going manner with the natives, is not 'man' enough to be a success. There is thus a sense in which, in order to colonize other races successfully, the white man has also to 'colonize' his own emotional life, as Mary represses her 'darkness', thus turning it into a source of fear, because it could undermine power and control. These issues, central to feminism, are explored with increasing complexity throughout Lessing's fiction, taking on many different forms.

2

The Limits of Realism: *Children of Violence*

(i) *'Martha Quest'*

With *Martha Quest*, published in 1952, Doris Lessing began a sequence of five novels with the collective title, *Children of Violence*. She has described this sequence as 'what the Germans call a *Bildungsroman*',[1] again linking her work with the nineteenth-century realist tradition. The name of the eponymous heroine exemplifies that link: in her quest for values to live by, Martha is to be the critic of her age, yet also its representative, a child of her age, one of the 'children of violence'. But the sequence was written over a period of 17 years, and by the time Lessing came to write the final volume, she had changed direction. Even in *Martha Quest*, there are tensions between the novel's themes and the realist form which make such changes inevitable.

The possible nature of those tensions is evident in the novel's opening chapter, which draws attention to Martha's less typical aspect. Her visionary daydream lays the foundation for the four-gated city of Volume V, and introduces many of the themes of Lessing's later, fable-like fictions: 'There arose, glimmering whitely over the harsh scrub and the stunted trees, a noble city, set foursquare and colonnaded along its falling flower-bordered terraces. There were splashing fountains, and the sound of flutes; and its citizens moved, grave and beautiful, black and white and brown together' (p. 17). The vision is not of a return to

1. Author's Notes, *The Four-Gated City* (St Albans: Granada, 1972), p. 671.

pastoral innocence, but of a city, a man-made order, its geometry – 'foursquare' – expressing social and emotional harmony. Its children are 'many-fathered', expressing Martha's dissatisfaction with the conventional nuclear family structure. Black and white live harmoniously together in obvious contrast to Southern African society. The city is clearly then a product of Martha's personal and political experience, as well as belonging to a tradition of Golden Age Utopias. As this vision develops, a discordant note is introduced by the exclusion from the city of anyone Martha dislikes, an act as divisive as the ideology she claims to reject. However, this vision remains more than a focus for petty discontents, since it is later related to experiences of a more profound, and less self-indulgent nature. The 'terrible illumination' (p. 61) usually comes when Martha is not absorbed in self-analysis, bringing with it not heightened self-consciousness, but a 'slow integration' into a sense of unity. These moments offer illumination of an uncomfortable kind, awareness of a very radical alternative to her existing way of life. In so doing, Martha's vision therefore raises questions and introduces concepts which cannot easily be dealt with within the conventions of realist fiction.

The unique and challenging nature of Martha's visionary experience is highlighted by the contrast the novel establishes between Martha and the rigidly structured environments in which she is situated. Each of Martha's worlds – the farming community in which she grows up, the town to which she escapes, and the Sports Club which dominates the lives of white youth – is peopled by characters whose lives are governed by rigid, though unwritten and unspoken, codes of behaviour, constructed to deter the expression of either personal experience or unpalatable social and political realities. The older Quests hide from the realities of their poverty behind the myth that it is only temporary, just as they and their contemporaries conceal the realities of war beneath myths of heroism and pathos. They expect Martha to conform to the role of the adolescent, which can then be used to explain away her rebelliousness: they can thus deal with her non-conformity without having to be aware of her individual problems.

But the behaviour of the rebellious young is itself codified and governed by convention, nowhere more so than in the Sports Club, which functions as a parodic microcosm of the social structure of the Colony. In their rebellion against the older generation and the European tradition it represents, the members of the Club construct a world even more firmly entrenched in the prevailing ideology. Their obsessive use of the slang terms 'kid' and 'baby' is intended to convey an informal modernity alien to the older generation, and the youthful irresponsibility they espouse as their ruling value. In effect it only underlines their self-consciousness, their implicit awareness of the temporary licence granted them by their privileged and parasitic relationship to the establishment they feign to despise. The role of women in the Club is indicative of this ambivalence. Women have an explicitly maternal function, assuming responsibility for the welfare and behaviour of the boys. Venerated as 'madonnas' within the club, their favours demanded in grotesque parodies of courtship, their future roles as mothers and wives are both taken for granted and despised by the male members. Binkie Maynard, son of the magistrate, is used to reinforce the parodic nature of the club, where he exercises a magisterial function, orchestrating its sexual relationships and organizing its disorder. As 'guardians of public safety', he and his minions ensure that couples do not transgress the prescribed limits of emotional shallowness, and that conversation steers clear of any political or social realities. The background of black servants, objects both of abuse and of mocking camaraderie, reminds the reader that this indulged period of life is underwritten for club members by the knowledge that they will in time become members of a far more powerful club – the ruling white elite.

Martha, however, is no more a simple victim of an inadequate environment than was Mary Turner. Like Mary, Martha is fatally split. But while it becomes clear that her visionary self is that which is repressed, the existence of a conforming self is not so immediately apparent. For Martha's rational, conscious self pursues images of freedom and rebellion, which appear to infringe convention and the prevailing ideology. Martha's chosen role as rebel, intended to distance her from this ideology, can be seen as, in a sense, a product of that ideology. As we have seen, the individual's identity, within Western culture, is constructed through the acquisition of an awareness of differences fostered by a system of language which emphasizes such differences through its articulation of basically binary oppositions. Martha believes that to be 'herself', to be 'an individual', is to be different. Identity is experienced as a sense of difference from others, as opposed to a sense of identity with others. Her deeper desires to belong, for that lost sense of unity enjoyed by all infants and returned to Martha in her visions, is displaced onto a more superficial desire for social approval, for roles which will reflect back on her a valued image.

The part played by language – and thus by the ideology inscribed in that language – in constructing Martha's conscious desires is demonstrated by the influence on her of European literature. Martha rejects the English literary tradition on which she, like so many other children of English descent, was brought up, because the novels of 'Dickens and Scott and Thackeray and the rest' (p. 35) relate neither to her external surroundings nor her inner landscape. The inadequacy of the nineteenth-century novel as an agent of social change becomes apparent to her when she watches black prisoners through her window – all the 'indignation' of that literary form has apparently achieved nothing in her world (p. 184). The 'poetry of suffering' (p. 32) likewise arouses in her an easy sentimentality which she recognizes as false. Yet Martha is so imbued with that tradition that she constantly sees herself as a heroine in the 'romantic tradition of love' (p. 202) which determines not only her sexual expectations, but her romantic conception of her social and political destiny. Talk of war immediately evokes a picture of herself as 'a heroine in the trenches' (p. 185) and that same sentimentality she has determined to reject. The writers who seem to have something to say to her are those poets who offer reassurance that she is a unique individual with a conscience free to reject the injustice that she sees around her, who foster the illusion of the free subject. The role of 'rebel' that they offer thus in no way challenges the ideological bases of the social structure. For that ideology prompts individuals to believe they are subjects – the 'I' of their own discourse – who can freely act upon their own environment. But the subject is also the subject of – in the sense of subjected to – the language he or she uses, and thus of the values and beliefs inscribed in it. [2]

Martha's reading, therefore, contributes to the formulation of two alternative, but equally false, ideal images – the rebel and the romantic heroine. And because her 'rebelliousness' is so often compromised by her desire for recognition and approval, it tends to be displaced onto more socially acceptable goals, in particular the traditionally sanctioned goal of women, romantic love. There, her identity can most surely be confirmed by that which she is not, her womanhood being confirmed by male response. She desires to be 'claimed' and 'possessed' by a man, even while – intellectually – rejecting such attitudes, and feeling totally alienated from her lovers. This deep-rooted desire to belong is embodied in the image of the dance: each dance she attends puts her 'under a spell', making her feel at one with the other dancers physically and emotionally.

Martha's disappointment in men repeatedly drives her back to

2. I am drawing here on the theories of Louis Althusser, usefully outlined by Terry Eagleton, *Literary Theory: An Introduction* (Oxford: Basil Blackwell, 1983), pp. 171–3.

books, as more trustworthy guides to living. She is thus presented with a repetitive pattern of choices, between men and books. But this is in reality no choice, since neither men nor books can offer anything other than reaffirmation of those values her other self rejects. Both belong to the symbolic order, in which she, like Mary Turner, cannot find a satisfactory place. To be accepted in that order she must either accept a subordinate place as a woman, or identify with the male values inscribed in the symbolic order itself, surrendering those values she finds lacking in the men in her life and the order they represent.

Joss Cohen, who repeatedly lends Martha books, appears to unite in himself those twin sources of guidance – male wisdom and the written word – to which Martha alternately turns. Yet this dual role highlights the confusion of needs which is at the root of her dilemma. Her responsiveness to his political ideals and values is so involved with her responsiveness to him as a man, however understated, that the real strength of her commitment is always suspect. When he finds her a job which enables her to leave the farm and begin another life, this release is 'like the kiss of the prince in the fairy tales' (p. 217), shedding an ambiguous light on her rejection of conventional women's roles. Similarly, when Martha rejects Donovan, who most clearly represents the codes of the town, it is 'under the spell' of Joss. Away from his influence, her readiness to conform to the expectations of other men in her life indicates the instability of her identity. Her radical political stance begins to seem simply another instance of conformity – a woman's traditional desire for male approval.

The extent to which Martha's rebellion itself observes a kind of conformity, is evident from her relationship with her parents. Her arguments with them are occasioned as much by her hostility to them as parents as by her espousal of beliefs and ideas which she values for their own sake. Thus Martha finds herself defending Hitler in response to her parents' criticism of him as a social upstart. Because she cannot afford to recognize that she is 'all the same a Quest' (p. 34), she labels those feelings she prefers not to acknowledge as 'outside pressures', so as to be able to retain her concept of herself as rebel. This role therefore becomes an end in itself, rather than a means to an end. Unable to recognize how she is split, she proceeds with her ill-fated marriage to Douglas in reaction to her mother's hostility to it. Believing that she can remain herself – free and critical – whatever her outward behaviour might suggest, she relegates herself to the position of the licensed fool. Unwilling to compromise her precious sense of difference, the totality of her existence is a tragi-comic compromise.

Political commitment seems to offer the attractive possibility of 'belonging' – reading the *New Statesman*, she feels 'at home . . . one of a brotherhood' – but this feeling is repeatedly dissipated by personal contact with those who share her beliefs, characters like Jasmine and the other members of the Left Book Club. This kind of personality clash, however, appears to be a flimsy reason for rejecting the kind of collective political action which might provide a more positive outlet for her rebellious dissatisfaction with the existing system. Later novels in the sequence indicate specific historical reasons for Martha's final rejection of organized rebellion as a viable option. Her active involvement with radical politics leads consistently to disenchantment. The Left in Southern Rhodesia is shown to be in a state of paralysis – split over the issue of black nationalism and frustrated by the racism of the white trade unions. But in *Martha Quest*, the reasons for opting out of such involvement are more immediately related to the dynamics of the group – any group. This appears to threaten Martha's sense of integrity as an individual, her sense of truth, which she feels to be uniquely hers.

Living in a state of false consciousness by refusing to acknowledge the operation of ideology, Martha's intended rebellion is thus negated. She is involved in repeated acts of self-betrayal which vividly illustrate that operation. What gives the Cohens, on the other hand, a relative independence from the prevailing ideology is their Jewishness, which makes them outsiders, on the margins of that society, even outcast from it. As Doris Lessing's later narrative stances will indicate, it is only from the margins that any distance from ideology can be achieved, that any truly radical analysis can be undertaken. Their repudiation of racism and their affirmation of socialist principles are built on practical as well as theoretical understanding of the issues involved. In contrast, Martha is saturated with the 'principle of separateness' (p. 56), however hard she tries to reject it. She therefore represses the meaning of her visionary experiences and the values they embody, in order to live the life of the young woman of the town. Those values only exist as part of a secret self of which we hear no more until the final part of the novel. Disillusioned with the Sports Club, Martha resurrects her earlier experience as a touchstone against which to measure the truths offered by books, that 'other journey of discovery'. The ideal of relationship and unity which it gives her casts an ironic light on both her attempts to 'belong' and her attempts to be 'different'. The image of the veld which formed the background to her visions gives her a growing sense of exile in town. The 'frank embrace between the lifting breast of the land and the deep blue warmth of the sky' (p. 252) represents an ideal of union she has failed to find in any of her sexual relationships. The gulf between the visionary and the 'real', the repressed and the conforming self, appears unbridgeable.

In undermining the concept of individualism, the novel thus ultimately calls into question one of the basic premises on which the tradition of the *Bildungsroman* is based. Furthermore, this undermining of the European realist tradition operates at the formal as well as thematic level. Like *The Grass is Singing*, the novel opens in the realist style, using all those devices which *assume* familiarity on the part of the reader, thus creating the recognition that it implies. It begins with 'objective' external description. Each feature of the scene on the Quests' verandah is presented as part of an already familiar whole: phrases like 'that part of the verandah' and 'they had been there since lunchtime and would remain until sunset' imply through the use of selective detail and the past perfect tense that the narrator *knows* the whole situation, past and present, rather than draw attention to the process by which the author is constructing it. The very familiarity of this literary convention encourages the reader's growing sense of 'knowing', so that there is an easy movement from the specific detail to observations of a more general kind, 'one such afternoon' (p. 33) being used to illustrate the norm, the totality of the character's existence.

At many points the narrator is close to being the traditional omniscient narrator, proceeding from specific comments on individual details of character and situation not only to more general observations about her characters, but to observations about society, or even humanity, in general. The author's knowledge of her own creation is, by implication, a knowledge of Southern African society as a whole, and human life in general. Statements like 'such is the lot of the peacemakers' (p. 27) are typical of the kind of pronouncements for which realists have been criticized in recent years. The objection to this narrative stance is not simply that such propositions are debatable in themselves, but more seriously that, in laying claim to truth, they may lull the reader into accepting as equally true all the author's prejudices and assumptions. Such generalizations are often prefaced by words like 'for' or 'now' which imply that there are logical reasons for making them, so that they may disguise ideology as reality. However, these effects are not, I think, as clear-cut as is often implied. To the independent reader a phrase like 'there could be no doubt' often raises the very possibility of doubt. The critical reader is likely to register with some alertness such explicit expressions of a point of view.

A more serious objection, I think, is that this kind of narrative constructs a 'hierarchy of discourses', whereby the 'authorial' voice is inevitably privileged over that of any of the characters.[3] Events are presented from a single, unified point of view which limits the possible signification of the text. We can best identify the nature of the problem in *Martha Quest* by considering the function of irony in the novel. An ironic narrative can convey both understanding and judgement of the position it gives voice to, but the emphasis tends to fall on the judgement, the 'misguided' viewpoint being placed and evaluated within a 'wiser' overview. This can contribute to the kind of 'closed' reading already mentioned. As Catherine Belsey has pointed out, irony is 'no less authoritative because its meanings are implicit rather than explicit.[4] It depends for its effect on a basis of shared assumptions within which the ironicized object or attitude is placed, and according to which standards it is found wanting. As such it is the ally of ideology, because it recognizes and resolves contradictions from a position of security, from the assumption that writer and reader are agreed as to the flaws in the position being exposed. Such contradictions therefore no longer present a challenge to the reader's perceptions. In *Martha Quest*, the problem seems to me to be related to the novel's implied readership. The novel explicitly and implicitly criticizes Southern African society in that ironic tone which assumes a certain critical distance between the reader and that society. But the implied reader and the actual reader are not one and the same. Are we to assume, therefore, that the novel was written to be read by the converted? How differently would a conservative or right-wing South African read the novel? As a novel which is essentially critical of divisiveness, of the divisions between black and white, Boers and English, young and old, men and women, it nevertheless potentially engenders just such a complacent divisiveness in readers who – accepting the liberal assumptions of the narrative and therefore feeling themselves to be on the side of the angels – are able to enjoy a superior sense of detachment from the society under analysis.

However, it is precisely this taking refuge in one's confidence of being 'on the right side' without actually being committed to anything, which Doris Lessing draws our attention to in Martha, who is no more immune to the novel's irony than her social environment, so that – as with Tony Marston – there is an attempt to ironicize the point of view

3. See Belsey, *Critical Practice*, p. 40.
4. *Op. cit.*, p. 42.

that the narrative itself might be assumed to be taking. But if we look at the novel's presentation of Martha's visionary experiences, the limitations of irony become apparent. Her feelings and thoughts at such times are reported semi-ironically, in free indirect speech. Assuming detachment and objective, rational judgement in the reader, this ironic tone, so characteristic of English fiction has distinct consequences when applied to highly emotional or spiritual experience that is unusual in quality or intensity. It is all too easy for such experience to be relegated to the realms of the humorous or the embarrassing.

Moreover, Martha's visionary experiences tend to seem totally divorced from the rest of the novel. After their earliest occurrence in Part One, there is no attempt to keep them in the reader's mind. Yet much later in the novel, 'that experience' (p. 220) is referred to, the assumption being that it has not been forgotten, that this piece of information can easily be retrieved from the mass of information absorbed in the reading process. Clearly its unusual nature makes such an expectation not unreasonable, but we would surely expect it to have some reverberations, some associations perhaps at the symbolic level with the rest of the novel? This disjunction emphasizes, of course, the split between Martha's two selves, but also contributes to some marginalization of the visionary self.

Some interaction between the two levels of Martha's experience is suggested in an incident which illustrates the stylistic problem. After avowing, in her heightened perception of the unity of all life, that she will never again willingly destroy a living thing, Martha goes out and shoots a buck. While the juxtaposition of these two events is obviously ironic, the narration of the shooting is extremely complex, suggesting that such a simple irony is not the whole story. The action is described twice, the first time as a deliberate act on Martha's part, implying a conscious rejection of the meaning of her vision. The second time suggests the inadequacy of the first bald description, which fails to reveal the motives and feelings accompanying the act. It suggests instead the act was unpremeditated and instinctual, having a more complex relationship to Martha's non-rational self. This dual narrative implies the inadequacy of rational analysis to deal with non-rational experience, an awareness of the limitations of realism.

The novel thus raises the problem of how to make plausible a radical alternative to existing structures and values – an alternative that promotes the non-rational – in a text in which the analysis of those structures is so eminently rational, exposing as it does the irrational prejudices and codes of behaviour which support them. Rather than seeing this disjunction between the visionary and the real as a weakness, however, it should perhaps be seen as a strength, since it becomes a means of evading that closure of meaning which I have suggested is symptomatic of a certain complacency in realist fiction. Where, at the end of a traditional *Bildungsroman* we would expect a gradual convergence of the two subjects – the narrator and the subject of her study – so that the heroine achieves the state of knowledge of the reader and narrator, there is no such resolution here. All contradictions and complexities are not ironed out and smoothed over by the narrator's privileged wisdom. The novel's ending presents instead an almost explicit challenge to that tradition, working on the very expectations that it creates. The convention that nineteenth-century novels about young women centre on courtship and end in marriage is present throughout the novel as a social convention that Martha rejects, leading the reader to expect something different of her future. And yet the novel ends with her marriage, conforming to the most traditional of patterns in an ironic reversal of our expectations that emphasizes Martha's tragi-comic failure to sustain the role of rebel she had espoused in preference to the traditional one. But the narration of this event – 'there is very little to say about the wedding itself' (p. 268) – denies it any sense of significance, of climax and resolution, and emphasizes that Martha sees it only as an inconvenient though necessary prelude to a new phase of life, another attempt to escape the past. In her apparent conformity she asserts her non-conformity. The only significant detail given – the fact that she was atrociously dressed but did not care – in a novel where her dress consistently expresses her willingness to conform to someone else's image of her, opens up some room for questioning, however ironically coloured.

However, this brusque unemotional treatment of Martha's wedding is not simply an implied comment on the 'happy ending' convention, but a reminder of the wider social purposes of realism. For the primary significance of the marriage is asserted in a precise factual summary: 'In this manner, therefore, was Martha Quest married, on a warm Thursday afternoon in the month of March, 1939, in the capital city of a British colony in the centre of the great African continent' (p. 269). This places the private event in its socio-historical context. After the wedding, a group of drunk young male guests run down a black African, a reminder of the political realities which remain untouched by Martha's attempts to escape her own personal dilemmas. And it is not Martha who observes this act but Maynard, the functionary of the society Martha rejects, ironically showing the same awareness of self and society that she believed belonged to her alone. The implied continuity between the two characters at this point suggests the ease with which such inner awareness can become absorbed into the system. Furthermore, it is with Maynard's observations, not the wedding itself, that the novel ends, turning Martha's marriage into a representative act. He sees it not as an individual act of choice, but as symptomatic and doomed, a response to the threat of war hanging over Europe. Maynard's final regrets over never having any grandchildren echo the sense of sterility and lack of a future which his visions conjure up, so that personal and political, individual and representative experience are fused. This detachment from the novel's main protagonist, so as to emphasize the context which makes the individual experience typical, is characteristic of the European realist tradition, reminiscent of, for instance, Balzac's *Cousin Bette*.

But if this ending seems, in this respect, to conform to the realist tradition, providing a Southern African version which might answer some of Martha's objections to that tradition's remoteness from her own experience, it nevertheless raises a number of questions which indicate an ambivalence towards that tradition. There is, above all, no reference to Martha's visionary experiences and to the alternative values they offer. If we look to a novel's ending for some clue to its meaning, then we cannot overlook this absence, for it indicates the difficulty of showing – within the terms of the realist convention – the bearing of Martha's vision on the social analysis provided by the novel. Her vision remains largely non-social, apparently untranslatable into practical or social terms in spite of Martha's original conception of the 'golden city', and therefore does not fit obviously into the social and political terms of the novel's ending. It belongs to a different tradition, the tradition of myth and fable, which criticizes society from a very different and ultimately more radical perspective than that of conventional realism. And it is to this tradition that Doris Lessing turns in her next novel sequence.

The novel therefore both thematically and formally questions the tradition of which it appears to be part, undermining the concept of the unified, essential individual self which is central to humanism, and questioning the capacity of the realist tradition to deal with radical experiences that lie outwith the parameters of that humanism. Martha's sense of her own inability to bring about change, either personal or social, is the corollary of her dream of the Golden City, so far removed from existing reality as to be unattainable by any piecemeal approach. The impasse to which this view leads Martha appears to reflect a conflict of interests in the novelist herself. On the one hand, the novel expresses a deep concern with social reality and the need for political change; on the other, it suggests the need to look inwards, into the repressed imaginative, feeling capacities of the individual. The final volume of the sequence appears to offer a different way of resolving the disjunction. It moves towards a more metaphoric mode of writing, so that there is less tendency for the visionary alternative to be marginalized by the rationalist assumptions of a realist narrative. As Doris Lessing's novels become increasingly more metaphoric, they also become more challenging, since they demand greater efforts of interpretation by the reader.

(ii) The Four-Gated City

Published in 1969, after *The Golden Notebook, The Four-Gated City* shares with that earlier novel a preoccupation with non-rational areas of experience, and in particular with the kind of consciousness most people would describe as abnormal, if not mad. What in *Martha Quest* were isolated and elusive moments of extraordinary perception, unhappily disengaged from the rest of her experience, are here central to that experience and to the novel – the true goal of her 'quest'. Nevertheless, it seems more appropriate to discuss this last novel in the *Children of Violence* sequence here, since in form as well as theme it is a direct development out of the earlier Martha Quest novels.

Before discussing *The Four-Gated City*, however, a brief summary of the intervening novels in the sequence may be helpful. In *A Proper Marriage* Martha's marriage to Douglas Knowell is, in spite of the birth of their child, put increasingly under stress by her political activities. For wartime, and the arrival of numerous RAF men in the city, have led many left-wingers like Martha to think more seriously about advocating an end to the 'colour bar'. When Douglas, a conventional civil servant, reacts badly, Martha decides to leave both him and her daughter. *A Ripple from the Storm* traces Martha's involvement with a number of men with whom she is more politically in tune, the most important being Anton Hesse, a Jewish refugee and dedicated Communist. Martha marries Anton to save him from deportation as an enemy alien, and works for various Communist committees, but this marriage is also destined for failure. The unity of the Left breaks down too, with Anton and Martha's group becoming the smallest and least effective. In *Landlocked* Martha has her first really meaningful love affair, with Thomas Stern, another Jewish refugee, this time from Poland. Both he and Martha are actively involved with the natives, but Thomas dies of a fever, and the native strike which Martha helped to develop is brutally put down. Martha divorces Anton, who has abandoned much of his earlier radicalism, and – feeling increasingly out of place in her own country – prepares to leave for England, where the final volume begins.

Like those earlier novels, *The Four-Gated City* constructs a solid and specific historical reality, which shows striking similarities to Doris Lessing's account of her own arrival in London in her autobiographical *In Pursuit of the English* (1960). Unlike those earlier novels, however, the narrator's relationship with that reality is an outsider's. In coming to London, Martha is following the sickness of Southern African society to its source. As a visitor from the colonies, she stands explicitly on the margins, observing the 'centre' of that civilization which gave birth to her own. The narrative therefore achieves a more obvious critical distance. Free to cross the boundaries between the East and West End of London, Martha is alert not only to the seediness of postwar Britain, in both its richer and poorer areas, and to the dampness which contrasts so strongly with the dry continent she has just left. She is also conscious of aspects of behaviour and mood which recall to her descriptions she has read of Britain in the 1930s. The early chapters of the novel explore the ideology of 'a country absorbed in myth' – contradictory myths of a society that is classless and yet on the verge of revolution. Her contact with the middle classes, Henry Matheson, talks about this classless society in the language of class-consciousness. Attempting to describe a girl in his office without explicitly referring to her social status, he uses phrases like 'She was *only* . . . her father was *under* me during the war, a very *good type* of man . . . you really can hardly tell her from . . .', all implying a rigid social stratification (p. 39). Whereas the boundaries that existed in Southern Africa were clearly visible – white and non-white – these boundaries are more insidious because invisible. The ugliness of the situation is illuminated by Martha, who sees both classes as 'savages' (p. 41): as an outsider she is vulnerable, unprotected in either world unless she is prepared to become one of them.

When Martha moves into the bizarre household of Mark Coldridge, a wealthy writer, the situation changes dramatically. However, Martha remains an outsider. To all intents and purposes free from family herself, she is in a position to 'diagnose' the condition of family life here. But the Coldridge household cannot be called an average family. Martha's services are required because Mark's wife, Lynda, is mentally ill and unable to look after their son, Francis, who has thus never known any normal mother–child relationship. When Mark's scientist brother defects to Russia, and his wife Sarah, a Jewish refugee, kills herself, another child is added to this family group. Paul, like Francis, is one of the new generation of 'children of violence', deprived of normal childhood experience and therefore unable to form 'normal' family relationships. These children are symbolic of a whole, damaged generation, a symptom of the sickness at the centre of the Empire.

Because Doris Lessing's social analysis is so convincing in its detail, the reader is drawn unsuspectingly towards the point at which the novel takes off into prophecy. A society in which nothing works properly, in which young people are disillusioned with politics and turn either to violence or alternative societies, in which the needs of industry override everything else, and in which even getting a fridge mended becomes a nightmare of procrastination and delay – the society of the 1960s – is a vision to which the contemporary reader's experience gives ready assent. It does not require a great leap of the imagination – post Chernobyl – to follow through from this scenario to the nuclear accident with which the novel ends. The ground is prepared when Mark covers his study walls and ceiling with newspaper cuttings, maps and other evidence of the gradual breakdown and growing insanity of society, evidence also of the links between these apparently disparate items. Whatever takes place in the realm of local or world politics, Mark here charts what is really happening, opposing his vision of 'reality' to the myths created by those in power, and sustained by those who cannot bear to face up to the truth. Here is the route map indicating the path to destruction in very precise detail, giving time, date, and place, providing statistics and fact such as the realistic novel has always relied upon to create its sense of verisimilitude. The novel's prophetic ending, however non-realist in the conventional sense, follows the inner logic of the text, and grows out of these guarantees of authenticity.

However, the novel moves even further in the direction of science-fiction in the 'Appendix', which focuses on the mutants born after the accident. Some of them display telepathic powers, highly developed forms of faculties of which Martha had been fleetingly aware during her visionary experiences. She describes these children as 'our guardians': it is as if they have lived through, survived and absorbed all the violence and horror of which man is capable, and emerged with a 'gentle, strong authority' (p. 662). One of them, Joseph, tells Martha that one day the whole human race will be like him, an advanced evolutionary form replacing all previous inadequate models. This vision of a post-apocalyptic new Eden clearly belongs to the realm of myth, and it is hard to avoid feeling that there is a slight suggestion that a nuclear accident might, in the long run, be beneficial. But the novel does not end on this optimistic, and to many readers whimsical, note. When Joseph is sent to Nairobi, to a rehabilitation settlement, he is classed as subnormal, 'fit for third grade work' (p. 664). Mark comments that 'the human race is united at last', but 'all busily looking into each other's faces for marks of *difference*' (p. 666). The challenging implication here is that violence, instead of being irrational, is a product of man's *reason*. For Western humanists, reason is the measure of all things: what is 'unreasonable' or 'irrational' is by definition undesirable, wrong-headed. However, such a belief rests on a divisive system of thought which attributes value to one thing only at the expense of something else, repeatedly turning difference into opposition and conflict. Apparently innocent, value-free contrasts like big/small, light/dark, man/woman, white/black, all too easily lead on to ideologically loaded pairings like major/minor, good/evil, masculine/feminine, Aryan/non-Aryan, white/non-white. Violence is in this novel seen as a consequence of man's obsessive use of 'reason' to differentiate and divide, whether racially, sexually, politically or physically. The challenge to rationalism is more explicit than ever.

This 'prophetic' shift can be seen as the result of the influence of Sufism, a form of Islamic mysticism which provides a kind of answer to that splitting of the self which I have suggested is central to Doris Lessing's presentation of her central characters.[5] The Sufis claim that ordinary people are capable of experiencing a higher working of the mind, transcending ordinary limitations, through which humanity can proceed to a higher level of evolution. Because enlightenment is to be achieved by working with the material world, Sufism aims to reconcile the spiritual and the practical, the irrational and the rational, the unconscious and the conscious. It thus offers the possibility of a unified self, and restores visionary experiences like Martha's to a valued and integrated role in life. In middle-age, therefore, Martha is able to look back over her past and see her various selves as mere variations on her 'real' self, her permanent self, to use a Sufi term. This core of being is represented in the novel by the individual's eyes – the only part to

---

5. Idries Shah, *The Way of the Sufi* (Harmondsworth: Penguin, 1974) is probably the most accessible introduction to the subject for those who wish to pursue it.

remain visibly unchanged, the traditional windows of the soul. Martha's awareness of her own permanent self remains elusive, but she comes closer to realizing it once she recognizes its basis in her childhood self. On her arrival in London, those early experiences of heightened awareness return, so that she sees herself in 'the lit space . . . Her mind was a soft dark empty space. That was what she was . . . a soft dark receptive intelligence' (p. 48).

But developing this 'Intelligence' requires a readiness to go beyond ordinary experience, as Martha learns through her developing relationship with Lynda. The two women use their dreams and fantasies as a first stage, as 'maps' to the territory that lies outside normal experience. Going through this 'door' makes the 'machinery of ordinary life' seem absurd and a trap (p. 508), a feeling Martha remembers from childhood, but had forgotten, as she finds she has forgotten so many vital experiences and early intimations of telepathic power: 'like any neglected faculty, it fell into disuse, it atrophied' (p. 525). Like other mystical texts, the novel reverses the usual associations of sleeping and waking, suggesting – to use Wordsworth's familiar phrase – 'our birth is but a sleep and a forgetting'. Martha and those around her have to struggle repeatedly to recall what their waking selves, education and society reject as nonsense. The achievement of a sense of unity with the natural world, the sense of seeing life again properly is moreover a mixed blessing since it brings with it a sense of the ugliness of 'normal' people, and a sense of alienation from them.

But, although Martha achieves enlightenment through a kind of mental breakdown, to which she deliberately submits herself alone in an empty flat, and with Lynda in her basement 'hell', this does not signify a rejection of reason in itself, only of an over-reliance on rationalism to the exclusion of all other philosophies. In order to learn from and survive these very frightening experiences, Martha needs every ounce of her analytical intelligence. Detachment is necessary for self-analysis as much as for social analysis. Martha's ultimate aim is not to live as a mystic, or in a mental asylum, but to return to everyday life. The activity of the Sufi connects and balances all areas of experience – understanding, being and knowing. 'This is the Work. Start with yourself, end with all.'[6] Sufism is 'not contemptuous of the world – "Be in the world, but not of it" is the aim.'[7]

Nevertheless, while Sufism offers the possibility of a unified self, that

6. See N.S. Hardin, 'Doris Lessing and the Sufi Way' in A. Pratt and L.S. Dembo, eds., *Doris Lessing: Critical Studies* (Wisconsin: University of Wisconsin Press, 1974), p. 150.
7. Lessing, 'In the World, Not of It', *Small Personal Voice*, p. 133.

splitting of the self which characterizes Doris Lessing's earlier novels remains as a shadow haunting Martha's quest. That splitting is less explicit, though in a sense more forceful, because in this novel Martha's two selves are projected onto the figures of Mark and Lynda, both functioning as Martha's alter egos. Their marriage is based on a deep sense of unity, but they are unable to live together, metaphorically signifying how potentially riven Martha's two selves remain. Husband and wife, moreover, represent the gender-based choice of identification which each individual makes in infancy. The nature of the choice is made starkly clear in the contrasted lives of Mark, the writer, and Lynda, confined to the basement with her bizarre assortment of companions – all social misfits. But Martha joins Lynda in exploring 'the walls of her own mind', thus breaking down the barriers between 'them' – those she had previously labelled as mentally ill – and 'us', asserting her identity with Lynda and her kind.

The identification between Martha and Mark is articulated by Martha herself in her recognition that he is going through the same political crises, conversions and disillusionment as her younger self (p. 193). Her creative consciousness also finds vicarious embodiment in his writing: his first short story, *A City in the Desert*, is about the destruction of the 'mythical city' (p. 150) of the novel's title. Some months later Mark rejects this novel as 'ivory tower rubbish', under the influence of his new role of 'the Defender', a conversion in which he takes on the position which Martha herself had held before coming to the Coldridge household. He attempts to revise the original cool detached account, making wildly emotional additions on the grounds that the earlier account lacked 'life' or 'guts'. But the narrator comments that ' "life" not to mention "guts" had no place in that story' (p. 194) – a clear conflict between myth and realism appears to be emerging, in which the ideals represented by Martha's early visions are being marginalized as irrelevant to the 'real' world. Is Martha's creativity in effect being compromised by Mark's use of language, of the symbolic order?

Mark's next piece of fiction, a proletarian novel, is a deliberate rejection of his first. *Working Hands* only runs to two chapters and is appallingly bad, but written from pure conviction, an expression of Mark's new-found political position. By the time *A City in the Desert* is published, so much has Mark's position changed that he has mixed feelings about its success, fulfilling as it does the requirements of the Cold War 'Ivory Tower' mood of the times. He next attempts to fictionalize the true-life story of Rachel and Aaron, which he found in the manuscripts of Thomas, Martha's former lover. But this novel, as full of anger and emotion as *A City in the Desert* was free of it, is never finished. Instead Mark produces *The Way of a Tory Hostess*, a series of sketches about his mother's country house, written when much younger. Inevitably this book is received as evidence that Mark has become a reactionary. The demand now is for books of commitment – Mark's career has not synchronized with the changing political and intellectual climate. Even his dramatized version of the Rachel/Aaron story, which satisfies the demands of literary critics for progressive writing, fails to satisfy the theatre critics who have *not* yet changed.

In America, however, *A City in the Desert* is published and received enthusiastically – by science fiction enthusiasts. While Mark and his novel barely change, after his 'conversion', the way that they are read does. The novel is always marginalized, seen as Ivory Tower escapism or science fiction fantasy. The prevailing ideology re-writes his texts for him whenever they are perceived as a threat. In contrast, when Jimmy Wood, Mark's inventive employee, begins to publish space fiction, containing the same ideas about para-normal powers that Martha and Lynda are exploring, his books sell in vast numbers, but are unread by intellectuals; no-one dreams of looking for the 'truth' in their pages. Mark finally abandons fiction, writing instead his Memoranda to himself, surrounded by charts, figures and maps which provide ample proof for him as to the future, but which most other people choose to regard as fantasy. In his writing career he has produced fantasy, social realism, emotional drama, light fiction, none of it read as it was intended to be.

It is obviously tempting to see this as in some way reflecting Doris Lessing's feelings about the reception of her own fiction.[8] But because Martha is not herself the novelist, there is less danger of the reader identifying her as the voice of Lessing herself. There is a degree of detachment from the heroine, a shifting point of view. For the first time in the whole sequence we see events from the viewpoint of her mother, formerly identified as the enemy, an extraordinary shift of emphasis unimaginable in the earlier novels in the sequence. The effect is to suggest that the lives of Martha and her mother follow the same fundamental patterns. Old age is a 'disguise' (p. 277), imposed on the 'real self' just like any other. Similarly, the novel ends with the voice of Francis Coldridge, one of the new generation. Martha's presence is only felt in letters from the wilderness on the fringes of civilization. Her voice is now truly speaking from the margins.

8. See her Preface to *The Golden Notebook*.

If the reconstruction of society falls on Francis's shoulders rather than Martha's, does this mean that we should regard Martha as an eccentric visionary, still unable to integrate properly with the ordinary 'real' world? Are her ideals irrelevant and romantic, or even conservative, as Mark implies in describing her city as 'hierarchic'? Francis's account, framed in factual, unemotive language, and with none of the weight that inevitably accompanies events seen from the perspective of the central protagonist, validates Martha's visionary intimations. She is vindicated through her acceptance by the younger and more prosaic generation, thus halting the cycle of rejection and rebellion which has throughout the sequence characterized the relationship of one generation to another.

For this volume puts more emphasis on the individual's responsibility for his or herself and others. As Martha herself asks, 'are we just children, and not responsible at all, ever, for what we live in?' (p. 296). No longer simply a daughter of the revolution, a child of violence, Martha is forced into the role of the middle-aged manager of a large household, 'forced back into that place in oneself where one watched' (p. 367), and by observing how the young around her are 'earlier versions of oneself' (p. 368), enabled to see that the process of working through and against one's heritage is not simply the experience of the unique, special person she thought herself to be, but an inevitable and necessary part of growing up. Martha notices the different personalities, past and present, of the Coldridge household becoming merged – Francis becomes 'Matty', her own younger self; Paul becomes Sarah – each generation going through the same experiences and mutations as the last, because one can only learn through experience: 'You start growing on your own account when you've worked through what you're landed with. Until then, you're paying off debts' (p. 468). Young Martha Quest had used 'any weapon fair or foul to survive', as everyone has to, but once the adult Martha has paid her debts to the past, and is in her turn besieged by the demands of the young, she is set 'free . . . from her personal past' (p. 401).

But this 'evolution' is clearly not an easy or straightforward one, even for those like Martha ready and willing to accept the evidence of her senses and the non-rational areas of her experience. As she learns to recognize and 'tune into' this universal consciousness, this 'impersonal current' or 'sea', she realizes that it 'could become the thousand volts of hate as easily as it could become love' (p. 511). Not only does she need to learn to contain this vast force, but she needs to defend herself against the 'self-hater' which could destroy her sanity. 'Impersonality' enables Martha to face and 'recover' her past, so that she is able to become whole – without this defensive retreat she is swallowed up by pain and self-pity. She must be able to feel an experience without being destroyed by it. But this is not the only difficulty: the other is the recurrent forgetting of all that has been learned. One cannot learn before experience has made one receptive, therefore 'timing' is vital for the success of the growing principle in life – a process of developing different 'ears', senses, with which can be heard what could not be before. It is in this area that the 'mutants' of the Aftermath show a distinct evolution: they appear able to shortcut this process, eliminating the need to experience and able instead to tap directly into the collective experience of humanity. Apparently backward because of their poor command of language – the symbolic order inscribed with the old values – they have extraordinary telepathic powers. Martha asks, 'I wonder how many small children in the old days had this capacity but lost it because they were laughed out of it or punished for "telling lies"?' (p. 660).

While I have suggested that the novel does not reject the use of reason, it does therefore highlight the limitations of rationalism, and of cultures that are totally rationalist. As scientists have observed, there are two sides to the brain – the left which is analytical, rational and verbal, and the right which is holistic, intuitive and spatial. Western civilizations have tended to encourage the left side, only allowing for the existence of the other through the clearly defined area of religion. This novel suggests it is time to modify such one-sidedness, which can also be seen as symptomatic of patriarchal habits of thought. In appropriating reason and knowledge as useful for the maintenance of power, Western man has marginalized the tenderer and more emotional dimensions of the psyche, labelling them 'feminine'. His binary discourse has created oppositions between activity/passivity, head/heart, for instance, which have been made to correspond with the oppositions man/woman, erecting a hierarchy in which the 'feminine' is always negative and powerless. Just as individuals, like Martha, forget their earliest intuitive experiences under the pressure to conform to adult patterns, so mystics like the Master Rumi of Balkh warn that 'civilized man' as he evolves forgets the 'earlier forms of intelligence . . . he has fallen asleep . . . He says "My sleeping experiences do not matter." ' (p. 461). Its potential evolution being thus delayed, society has reached the point where it is unable to exercise even its rational powers and is 'unable to think' or to 'diagnose its own condition' (p. 465). All it can do is label and compartmentalize anything unknown or potentially threatening, simply to stop the process of thought. Given such social organization, truth can perhaps only be found in 'madness', in the margins.

The ideal of the four-gated city then, if not to be achieved through changed social organizations, retains significance at the end of the sequence, representing as it does the lost unity of individual and environment. The prerequisites for this perfect city are 'Freedom' and 'order', apparently irreconcilable within the binary system of logic to which we are accustomed. The novel therefore appears to advocate the Sufi view that we must change the inner consciousness before society, shifting away from the Marxist view that social and economic change must come first. Indeed, the novel seems to suggest that the necessary social changes are simply not possible. Any hope Martha might have had of finding a solution in collective political action has been abandoned: if people like Phoebe, a committed and active Socialist, 'could not put their faith in "the people" there was nowhere to put it. Yet what "the people" supported during those years was a [Tory] government more corrupt and ineffectual than any in the history of this country' (p. 493).

But if mysticism thus seems to be a logical option for Martha, given the nature of her earlier experiences, is it a convincing universal solution? Is the psychological plausibility of the individual case, the constructed reality of the character's experience, being used to impose an ideology? For Sufism clearly comes into the category of ideology, yet is never subjected to the same scrutiny as other ideologies in the text. There are many readers who feel that this turning away from political commitment towards the inner life is a form of reactionary romanticism, which simply overlooks the political options. While Doris Lessing admits to being less 'progressive' than she used to be, in the sense of rejecting the ethos of material and technological progress, it is hard not to feel that this aspect of her writing lays her open to being deemed less progressive in a broader, more critical sense.

Finally, this vision of a future in which hope lies with individuals who are able to communicate without speech, and who are distinguished by what they share rather than what differentiates them, raises questions which are more fundamental to realist fiction than the obvious ones of credibility, for it runs counter to the highly individualistic perspective of realism. Similarly, the process undergone by Martha – her 'setting free into impersonality' (p. 401) – involves the loss of what we normally conceive of as identity, the surrender of her belief in individuality, in a subjectivity privileged by its uniqueness, whereas we expect the resolution of a *Bildungsroman* to provide the central character with a highly developed sense of self. What are the implications for characterization if the writer pursues this quest for what is 'impersonal' in people? We may find fuller answers in Doris Lessing's second novel sequence. What is already clear is the extent of her reaction against the realist tradition. This novel insists on the need to go beyond the here and now to construct an alternative image of reality.

3

The Golden Notebook and Reflexive Form

The publication of *The Golden Notebook* in 1962 marked the change of direction which I suggested took place before Doris Lessing finished writing the *Children of Violence* sequence. Lessing has referred to spending the last twenty or thirty years in the company of people who could be described as 'mad' in various ways, an experience causing her to depart from her earlier 'atheistic, progressive and rationalistic' position.[1] She has further stated that she was only able to write about her heroine's breakdown after she herself had accidentally gone without food for several days. As a result, parts of the novel were written on a 'different level' from any of her earlier work.[2]

Nevertheless, Doris Lessing's Preface to this novel shows the same concerns as those expressed in her 1957 essay. One is that it was not at that time possible to find a novel which described the intellectual and moral climate of Britain in the middle of the last century in the way that Tolstoy did it for Russia, and Stendhal for France. This almost sociological approach to the novel was reiterated in a television interview Lessing gave in 1980, in which she spoke of writing for people living in a hundred years time, as if writing a 'historical novel', to use Lukacs's term.[3] Lessing articulates this view in the novel itself, using a novelist,

1. Quoted in C.J. Driver, 'Profile', *New Review*, I (1974), p. 20.
2. 'Interview with Roy Newquist', *Small Personal Voice*, p. 60.
3. Georg Lukacs, *The Historical Novel* Trans. H.&S. Mitchell (London: Merlin Press, 1962), pp. 19–30.

Anna Wulf, as protagonist. Anna's work as a reviewer leads her to conclude that the modern novel 'has become an outpost of journalism; we read novels for information about areas of life we don't know . . . We read *to find out what is going on.*' This idea is very familiar to readers of nineteenth-century Realist fiction. The 'condition of England' novel of the 1840s aimed to make the 'two nations' of England, rich and poor, more aware of each other, while for writers like George Eliot the novel's primary moral function was the extension of the reader's sympathies through the elimination of ignorance and prejudice. Anna similarly sees the originality of modern novels lying in the fact that they record 'the existence of an area of society, a type of person, not yet admitted to the general literate consciousness' (p. 79). The novel has become for her a function of the fragmented society and the fragmented consciousness: readers are grasping for information which will make them feel whole.

But *The Golden Notebook* also demonstrates that distrust of Realism as a series of conventions which I have suggested characterizes Doris Lessing's fiction. Anna repeatedly comments on the limitations of the traditional novel, on the impossibility of conveying 'reality' through that form, and indeed casts doubts on the nature of that 'reality' to which nineteenth-century fiction was committed. Writing with a twentieth-century consciousness of relativity and the philosophical problems associated with determining what constitutes reality, Anna is aware that the only 'reality' the individual can be sure of is his or her subjective perception of it: for the modern writer, as Lessing herself puts it, there is 'no way of *not* being intensely subjective' (Preface, p. 13). However, both Anna and her creator argue that any novel about individual human emotions must in turn reflect external reality, since these emotions are a product of society (p. 61). If subjectivity itself is a social construct, any exploration of the processes by which it is constructed will be an implicit analysis of the dominant ideology of that society.

This relationship between the subject and ideology is what makes it possible for the novel to function both as a 'historical novel', satisfying the traditional concerns of realist fiction, and as a highly innovative account of individual subjectivity. The novel can moreover simultaneously be read as 'about' novel-writing, an example of what has become known as reflexive form, since it both thematically and formally, explicitly and implicitly, raises questions about the nature and function of the novel, without being exclusively concerned with literary production. It is probably because of this thematic and formal complexity that many critics consider this novel to be Lessing's finest.

The Golden Notebook's critique of Realism is evident in its very structure. It consists of sections entitled 'Free Women', which represent a 'conventional' novel. Each section is followed by extracts from four notebooks intended to indicate how much of 'life' the conventional novel leaves out: 'a black notebook, which is to do with Anna Wulf the writer, a red notebook, concerned with politics; a yellow notebook, in which I make stories out of my experience; and a blue notebook which tries to be a diary' (pp. 461–2).

The Black Notebook, headed 'The Dark', is itself further divided into entries under the headings 'Source' and 'Money', the first introducing memories of Anna's African experiences, the 'source' of her first novel *Frontiers of War*. The second covers the financial transactions relating to this very successful novel. After a few pages, the entries on the left cease, the source of her inspiration apparently drying up, while the commercial transactions continue busily for three years. The Red Notebook, firmly and precisely headed 'The British Communist Party', lacks the hesitations and divisions of the black. It is precisely dated January 3rd 1950, and the double underlining of the heading suggests a firmness of purpose, which Anna hopes to find in political commitment. The Yellow Notebook 'looked like the manuscript of a novel' (p. 177), although Anna claims to be suffering from a writer's block. Ella, the heroine of *The Shadow of the Third*, is a fictionalized projection of Anna's self and situation. The Blue Notebook begins 'Tommy appeared to be accusing his mother' – Tommy being the son of Anna's closest friend, Molly – and continues as a kind of diary, including extracts from an earlier diary of 1946 – a diary within a diary, as *The Shadow of the Third* is a novel within a novel, so that we experience the author as reader as well as writer of her own work, an activity of considerable importance in indicating how we, the readers, might carry out this activity.

For Anna, the author, draws the reader's attention to the limitations of the Notebooks themselves. The first time that she reads them through, she feels they are completely untruthful, in spite of her hope that they would do the fullest justice to the varieties of her experience. Each acts as a different *version* of 'reality'.

Every version of 'reality' is, then, encoded in a discourse, a way of representing experience which is formulated in relation to particular sites of language use, and which operates in accordance with its own conventions. In *The Golden Notebook* the reader is confronted by literary discourse, psychoanalytic discourse, political discourse, and the discourse of sexual relationships. The problems experienced by Anna in attempting to formulate her experience in terms of these varied discourses demonstrates the way that language constructs the subject, each discourse tending to fix Anna in a specific subject position, which is always a marginalized one: a woman, an artist, an ex-colonial, Left-wing in politics, who experiences the extreme margins of mental break-down. Anna and her friend Molly, the protagonists of the ironically titled *Free Women*, are 'free' in so far as they are sufficiently independent of family, financial constraints, and social and moral institutions to be freely critical of those same institutions. But that very independence, their position as outsiders, in effect silences them, or ensures that they will not be listened to to any purpose. As Doris Lessing says in her Preface, the marginalizing process ensures that people with an original or reforming streak will effectively be eliminated from any position of power or importance. In an attempt to be *more* truthful, she uses the Blue Notebook purely as a record of facts, as if she 'Anna, were nailing Anna to the page' (p. 462). She sees herself as thus saving each day from chaos.

Through language, as we have seen, the subject is constructed as split. And the multiplicity of discourses within *The Golden Notebook* is a manifestation of that splitting which is a central theme of the novel. Even in personal, sexual relationships, where we might expect to come closest to a 'real' or 'essential' self, we find a discourse which constructs the self in terms of the most fundamental binary oppositions. Anna's notes for a new novel, *The Shadow of the Third*, written in the Yellow Notebook, describe the splitting process involved in constructing sexual identity. The shadow figure is the 'third' in Ella's relationship with her lover, Paul. Originally it is Paul's wife: Ella imagines her 'in her own shadow, everything she is not' (p. 212). Her fear of losing Paul's love creates in her a sense of lack which in turn creates a corresponding desire to change, to conform to this imaginary, shadowy ideal in order to regain his love and approval. She thus begins to hide her work from him, silencing part of herself, because it incurs his disapproval. He believes her too ignorant and naive to write about suicide, to encroach on his expertise as a psychiatrist. That is, he rejects personal experience and its discourse as an inappropriate source and medium for writing about his professional domain, a domain in which he possesses 'knowledge', and authority. This aspect of Ella's relationship provides an idea for a short story – a woman has a new personality created for her by her lover when she becomes everything he criticizes her for being, although she was none of these things. Finding he loves the creation she becomes, she realizes he has rejected her real self.

Men are thus depicted in the novel as 'naming' women, using the language of the patriarchal order to define and thus limit women, and the ideological process described in Chapter 1 of this study ensures that women, in turn, collaborate in this process. Anna responds to Saul, her American lover, because he 'named' her on a high level (p. 534). Ella sees this as an explanation for the frequency with which 'nice' women fall in love with men who are unworthy of them: they fall in love with those men who 'name' them, who give them a distinct and authorized sense of identity (p. 516). Furthermore, Anna claims a woman's sexuality is 'contained by a man, if he is a real man' (p. 443): her desire itself only comes into being in response to the man she loves, and is constructed by the figure who exercises this emotional control over her. At the end of every relationship, therefore, a woman has to 'recover' herself, to revive the self that has been repressed in that particular relationship. At the end of her five-year affair with Michael, Anna has to use 'the critical and thinking Anna', the side of her he liked least (p. 327) to restore what she conceives of as her identity.

Therefore, while women too appear at times to assume an authoritative role in 'naming' men, this authority is deceptive, merely a temporary borrowing of male authority which reinforces patriarchal values. The mirror-image of the desire to submit which is a product of patriarchal ideology is this desire to 'create' men, 'real' men. Anna perceptively labels this a 'negative' desire (p. 470). Consciously or unconsciously she appears aware that women are constrained by the language available to them, inscribed with patriarchal values, which ensures that a 'real' man can only be conceived of in opposition to a 'real' woman – dominant to her passivity. Anna's firm exclusion of homosexuals from her definition of 'real' men suggests a surprisingly essentialist view of gender, of what is 'truly' male and female, and this has led many recent feminist critics to reject earlier views of the novel as a feminist manifesto before its time. Such critics regard Anna's apparently traditional view of her sexual identity as a betrayal of those aspects of life which should properly concern feminists. But it is firstly a mistake to see Anna's views and feelings as an authoritative expression of the author's views, going unchallenged by the rest of the text – a point I shall return to. Secondly, the text is not so much concerned with how feminists do or should live, as with demonstrating the processes by which a woman's sense of self is constructed, which – within the society which Doris Lessing depicts – involves a perception of self in sexual and emotional relationship to men. Ella, for instance, is only too aware that her emotional dependence on men does not equip her for the kind of life that, intellectually and theoretically, she sees herself as living – the life of the liberated woman. But that subjectivity is neither freely chosen on her part, nor essential and instinctive. It is, as we have seen, a social construct. As such, the process is one by which men too – though arguably in a more beneficial sense, which enables them to maintain their power – are subjected to ideology. Paul, for instance, is similarly fragmented: he is capable of laughing at his own professional discourse – the discourse of psychoanalysis – telling the same stories in 'the language of literature and of emotion' (p. 214). Split himself, he nevertheless resents Ella's attempts to link his three different personalities, her attempts to assume an authoritative, 'naming' role.

If even the intimate discourse of sexual relationships is inscribed with the values of the dominant party, reflecting a particular power structure, then we can expect such encoding to be even more evident in public discourse, particularly the political. Even when writing about the Left, whether in post-war Southern Africa, or in the Communist Party in Britain in 1957, Anna observes the same muting of the dissenting voice: 'the phrases of our common philosophy were a means of disguising' individual differences (p. 294). In 1957 Anna receives a series of letters from trade union officials, which are identical in phrasing, style and tone, all individuality being suppressed by the party discourse, the line – in this case the defence of Stalin. This set is followed by three condemning Stalin, in equally similar 'hysterical, self-abasing' terms (p. 68). Three more follow, the week after the Hungarian uprising, 'purged of doubt, stern and full of purpose', as if the second set had never been written. And because the individual voice is lost, the individual's 'truth' is also lost. Again the complicity characteristic of the ideological process is evident. Even Anna's American lover, Saul, a disillusioned ex-Communist, resorts in his eventual breakdown to a 'stream of parrot-phrases' which Anna can label 'Communist, American, 1954. Communist, English, 1956' (p. 570), or as appropriate. He uses what he would otherwise regard as gibberish because it provides a reassuringly familiar, valorized formula when his own sense of reality is shifting, unreal and frighteningly chaotic. Moreover, while two people may be able to discuss politics relatively honestly, the presence of a third is sufficient to create a group consciousness or loyalty, which silences individual doubts. In such a group, everyone speaks of Stalin, for instance, in a 'tone of simple, friendly respect' (p. 301), in spite of the suspicion that he is a mass murderer. When Anna finds herself stammering when refuting accusations about Stalinism, this linguistic disfunction is the first indication of a withdrawal of such public loyalty (p. 299). Similarly, although the 'first principles' of the South African Communist Party – that 'the proletariat was to lead the way to freedom' and that Black nationalism was a right-wing deviation – are leading nowhere, because they fail to acknowledge the reality of the white trade unionists' racism, such 'first principles' are 'too sacred to question' (p. 106).

Discourse can be defined therefore in terms of what it excludes, as much as by the assumptions which it includes. It simultaneously of course determines who is excluded from the group, who or what is marginalized because of their failure to subscribe to the language of the group. The discourse of a political party identifies the individual member with the group, at the same time defining that member as different from those who do not so belong. The sense of belonging, that is, can only be purchased at the cost of the exclusion of others. This process is inherent in group dynamics, even in those which claim to speak for those who have been marginalized: it becomes apparent to Anna that 'inherent in the structure of a Communist Party or group is a self-dividing principle', a process of centralism by which new margins will constantly be created (p. 85). This centre will, moreover, coalesce around those with least self-doubt, least ready to acknowledge the existence or validity of alternative views or positions, like Willi Rodde, the German refugee who becomes Anna's lover in the Black Notebook. Willi became 'centre' of a war-time communist sub-group in the Colony because of his 'absolute certainty that he was right' (p. 89). In retrospect, Anna feels that she and the others were locked in this group, which imprisoned thought as much as it provided a forum for originally 'marginal' social and political beliefs (p. 153). Even in the 1960s, Anna still finds herself being told by Party hardliners like her colleague Jack Preston that they 'must submit to being split' (p. 353). Just as entry into language produces a splitting within the psyche between the conforming self, desiring those socially approved goals and values inscribed in the language system, and the repressed self and its unacceptable desires, so access to a political discourse conferring group identity and approval involves the repression of individual dissent. Group members must therefore surrender the desire to judge what is 'right' for themselves. Like any institution, even the Communist Party exists by absorbing or destroying its critics through this endless process of marginalization.

The implications of this suspicion and suppression of the individual voice are serious for Anna, the writer. She herself has given lectures subscribing to the view that the best art of the past was communal, not possessed of the 'driving painful individuality of the art of the bourgeois era'. She too has looked forward to the day when art would no longer express 'man's self-divisions and separateness from his fellows' (p. 344). However, when she finds herself stammering while attempting to deliver these arguments, she is forced to recognize that such words belong to a specific ideological discourse, rather than to her own experience. Her own literary discourse has indeed been the object of this political discourse. In 1952, *Soviet Weekly* published reviews of her first novel, *Frontiers of War*, describing it as a courageous revelation of the injustices of the British Empire, but by 1956, critics term the same novel 'negative' and 'unhealthy', reflecting Stalinist demand for 'social' realism. The recurrent complaint this time is that the novelist should have found 'a solution, political, social, spiritual' to the racial conflict she depicts. 'Where are the working masses in this book? Where the class conscious fighters?' (p. 433). Here is one discourse challenging another. The critics of *Soviet Weekly* look for a discourse which will represent reality as it ought to be, not as it is according to Anna's perceptions.

Nevertheless, Anna's complicity in the ideological process is such that, believing the artist needs discipline, she partially accepts the demands of the party, hoping they will provide a sense of direction, and justification for an activity which she herself cannot wholly approve of (p. 81). As we found when considering Martha Quest's politics, the revolutionary Left, while appearing to provide an outlet for the most radical impulses, nevertheless satisfies the conforming self by conferring approval on conformity to the Party line. In her uncertainty, therefore, about the legitimacy of her own fiction, which she now perceives as falsifying in its nostalgia, as well as inherently self-indulgent, Anna attempts to erase her own subjectivity. Her Blue Notebook represents an attempt to come closer to objective 'reality' than she succeeded in doing in her first novel. But instead, these diaries raise doubts and questions about the 'reality' of even the Notebooks themselves. The reader had previously taken the Black Notebooks, for instance, to be a 'true' autobiographical account of Anna's African past. But her 1950 diary in the Blue Notebook contains extracts from a 1946 diary in which she refers to her first husband as Max Wulf – 'Willi' in the Black Notebook (p. 233). If names have been changed, what other changes may have occurred? Having read that the experiences described in this notebook formed the basis of Anna's first novel, the reader finds the line between reality and fiction even more blurred. The status of any of these versions of 'reality' becomes uncertain. Anna's attempts at recording the objective reality of her own existence in the Blue Notebook soon end, and the diary ceases to be any kind of personal document, being replaced instead with newspaper cuttings documenting the wars, violence and destruction which make the news from 1950 to 1954, and which she clearly feels constitute something more 'real' than her individual existence (p. 241). Later in the Blue Notebook Anna again attempts an 'objective' version of reality by summarizing the preceding pages of detailed description of her thoughts, feelings and activities in a single day in a single paragraph beginning 'A normal day'. This 'neat and orderly' entry (p. 360) is followed a month later by even briefer entries, 'short factual statements: "Got up early. Read so-and-so. Saw so-and-so" ', continuing for eighteen months (p. 455). But this too is deemed a failure, and scored through. The erasure of subjectivity brings us no closer to the truth.

The novel appears, therefore, to generate an opposition between political commitment on the one hand, and artistic integrity on the other, since political conformity seems to require the suppression of individuality. Is 'truth', therefore, to be found in artistic self-expression, or is this a false and simplistic opposition? Does art represent freedom, or is it simply another discourse? Since every discourse is inscribed with the values of a particular ideology, there appears to be nowhere for the individual voice to be heard. The notion of 'free speech', like freedom itself, is an illusion, as is the Romantic concept of the artist as the voice of the free individual speaking out against society's conventions and values:

> the child is taught that he is free, a democrat, with a free will and a free mind, lives in a free country, makes his own decisions. At the same time he is the prisoner of the assumptions and dogmas of his time, which he does not question, because he has never been told they exist. By the time a young person reaches the age when he has to choose . . . between the arts and the sciences, he often chooses the arts because he feels that here is humanity, freedom, choice. He does not know that he is already moulded by a system: he does not know that the choice itself is the result of a false dichotomy rooted in the heart of our culture. (Preface, p. 16)

The concept of freedom – artistic or otherwise – rests on the belief that there can exist a subjectivity untouched by ideology – free, autonomous and unified. When Anna does attempt to communicate a more 'subjective' reality, the initial results are as problematic as her attempts at objectivity, throwing the very existence of such a subjectivity into question. Anna attempts to explore the fullest depths of her subjectivity in conversation with the psychoanalyst she nicknames Mother Sugar. Through analysis, Anna hopes to overcome the divisions to which she is subject, to restore a sense of wholeness. Mother Sugar suggests that Anna's repressed subjectivity, which is being silenced by her refusal to write fiction, is speaking in her dreams, which have the quality of 'false art, caricature, illustration, parody' (p. 238), as if the repository of all her creativity. But while Anna may accept this analysis of the processes of repression, what she is ultimately being offered by Mother Sugar is simply another discourse – the language of psychoanalysis. Through psychoanalysis, she is forced back into myth, invited to 'fish among the childish memories of an individual' and merge them with the 'child-hood of a people' (p. 456). Being invited to 'name' a bit of chaos in terms acceptable to Mother Sugar, and give it form is like holding something safe in a story. By identifying it, labelling it, as an aspect of human experience in general, the individual puts the experience away from him or herself, is freed from it. What Mother Sugar does is to demand of Anna 'definition' (p. 251) of her experience, as if labelling it renders it non-problematic. She analyses Anna's dreams, translates them into rational discourse, familiar patterns, which again change their unique meaning for Anna just as surely as translating poetry into prose. Similarly, when she suggests that Anna should write a diary, as a step towards unfreezing her writer's block, Anna feels she is 'making it part of *her* [the analyst's] process', thus 'robbing' Anna of it (p. 241) The diary, like the dreams, will be appropriated into the discourse of psychoanalysis.

In an attempt to capture her individual subjective reality in her own terms, Anna sets out as truthfully as she can to record every thought and feeling for a single day – 17 September 1954 (p. 327). But the act of writing inevitably transforms the nature of any event or 'reality' it records, since it brings a consciousness to that experience which was not originally present. The result is a falsifying emotionalism. The most everyday event in life, she notices, becomes shock-producing in literature, whether it be Joyce's Leopold Bloom defecating or Anna menstruating. The shock is produced not by the nature of the event itself, but by the fact that it is being introduced into literary form; its recording makes more of a comment on other literature than on life. The inclusion of such events represents a challenge to existing literary codes which draws attention to the details disproportionate to their significance in her life. To speak where there had once been silence is not simply to fill in a gap, but to make that gap reverberate with the significance of the centuries of silence. To attempt a new discourse is inevitably to pass comment more on the nature of previous discourses than on reality itself.

Anna therefore acquires a growing suspicion of language, even though for her as a writer 'words are form' (p. 463). She finds all words become meaningless as her mental state deteriorates, as she loses touch with the 'thinking Anna' who 'can look at what Anna feels and "name" it' (p. 465). That act of naming, that imposition of form, is itself seen to falsify. Anna notices that, at the end of any experience, 'it falls into a pattern', so that any relationship is seen retrospectively 'in terms of what ends it'. As 'literature is analysis after the event', it will always falsify, in contrast with living, which is simply 'the physical quality of life' (p. 231). Anna's writer's block is inevitably linked to these doubts about the nature of language. It might, however, be more appropriate to think of this block as a self-imposed silence, in so far as Anna continues to write – in all her notebooks – but refuses to produce fiction for a reading public, to communicate with any reader. This feeling is evident at the very beginning of the first notebook, intended as a way through that block. The Black Notebook begins with 'doodlings, scattered musical symbols, treble signs that shifted into the £ sign and back again . . . then words' (p. 75). It is only as a last resort that Anna uses words as the only sign system available to her for her purpose. It is surely significant that those first doodlings employ musical signs, the language of the most abstract of all art forms, the language least likely to falsely imply any correspondence with 'reality'. These 'art' signs in turn shift into financial signs, for it is one of the novel's ironies that the novel which she now sees as such a falsification of its 'source' in her experience has become in another sense a source for her life, in so far as it provides her income. Hence Anna's attempt to divide off the 'money' from the 'source' entries – the discourse which signifies the entry of her words and experience into the public sphere from the discourse which attempts to revive the reality of the private experience.

Is there, then, no way beyond discourse – no way of using language which is not already inscribed with the ideological assumptions of a particular construction of reality? One possible answer is to attempt to subvert that discourse for one's own ends – to use parody, for instance, as a way of deflating and mocking its assumptions. Unwilling to adapt *Frontiers of War* for film, because she dislikes the de-politicizing commercialism and sentimentality enshrined in the discourse of the mass media, Anna writes instead parodies of film synopses. However, her agent tells her these would be accepted by the producers interested in her novel because they are 'written in their terms' (p. 78). Anna later writes imaginary journals by a sensitive woman writer, also intended as parody, but again accepted by her publisher at face value (p. 429). When her friend James Schaffer, a young American writer, produces a short story, *Blood on the Banana Leaves*, the very title of which is intended to signal its parodic nature, it is again unrecognized as such. Anna thus decides that parody has become impossible in her society. As long as a familar discourse is employed, readers will accept the representation of reality inscribed in it, without worrying about the relationship between that discourse and the 'truth' it is encoding. There is no way for the writer to control the way in which this discourse will be read, unless there exists a prior readiness in the reader to distance oneself from ideological practices. Or, unless the writer produces a context, a norm, against which the parody can be measured, which is in effect what the multiple discourses of *The Golden Notebook* provide.

This gap between surface meaning and authorial intent is, nevertheless, one which Anna sees endlessly exploited by those around her, as a means of letting unauthorized truths speak. Such truths often become evident within the discourse of political groups through irony, a form of discourse largely dependent on tone and inherently indirect, which thus avoids direct, explicit criticism. Among the pleasures which Anna admits to deriving from membership of the Party are the 'elaborate ironies and complicities of the initiated' (p. 165). Irony enables the speakers to acknowledge truths that the myths of their discourse prevent them from articulating publicly. It is a form of evasion which signals both clear-sighted integrity – 'I am honest enough to admit that the party line is not the whole truth' – and ultimate loyalty – 'but I will remain silent in order to protect the interests of the party, which are at the moment paramount.' No-one using this tone will have to defend what they say, since no-one else has to take their words seriously. As Freud suggested of jokes, by such means does the repressed reach the surface of consciousness, whether that of the individual or group. In a challenge to that first principle mentioned previously, Paul Blackenhurst delivers a statement in 'angry parody' of the group's usual discourse (p. 109): he suggests that, after any future conflict between black and white, the successful black nationalists would need to develop 'capitalist unegalitarian' ethics to strengthen their position, which even the Communist Party would have to support. A rare moment of truth thus enters into the group's conversation, without the representation of reality inscribed in their habitual discourse being in any way threatened.

But this kind of irony can operate with more destructive consequences in personal areas of life. Here it becomes clear that it is less an indirect means of telling the truth than an evasion of the truth, a refusal to acknowledge one's true feelings. Even in his relationship with Ella, Paul Tanner uses phrases which act as ironic shorthand comments on reality, evading whatever is most painful by cloaking it in humorous form. What he believes to be her infidelities become her 'literary lunches', her novel her 'treatise on suicide' (p. 214), his own jealous constructions of reality aptly manifesting themselves in further fantasy forms. In contrast, the emptiest relationships can be sustained by the adoption of a 'self-aware, self-parodying humour' that insulates against reality and pain: Anna observes a beautiful blonde at a party 'babying' her husband out of drinking too much. Irony and self-parody, in private as in political spheres, demonstrate a refusal of real commitment. By preventing others from taking the speaker seriously, they put barriers in the way of meaningful relationships. Valued as a form of sophistication, irony is in fact an expression of insecurity, since it implies distrust of even those with whom one supposedly shares close ties of affection or belief. In contrast to such 'sophisticated' forms of communication, Anna reflects on a code which she, as a novelist, would never use in her work, because such words 'mean nothing, when you start to think about them' (p. 123). But this language – words like 'nice' and 'good' – is used by everyone in the confidence that everyone else will understand it. It is linked with a quality which Anna calls 'naivety', in opposition to that sophisticated intelligence which is characteristic of most of the characters in the novel. As soon as Ella uses the word 'love' in her relationship with Paul, 'there is the birth of naivety' (p. 216), and Anna recognizes the same quality in her relationship with Michael. To love means to give birth to 'a spontaneous creative faith', existing in spite of the intellectual awareness of the probable end of that relationship. The alternative – entering into a relationship with intelligence totally in control – means entering into a 'deliberately barren, limited relationship'. Naivety is thus ultimately a creative force enabling a woman – for it is women who are shown to be in possession of this quality – to act *as if* her love will last forever, as it also enables the political idealist to pursue a vision, whatever political expediency might dictate as a wiser course of action.

Doris Lessing might appear to be sanctioning a naive acceptance of the status quo itself, of the assumptions inscribed in such terms as 'nice' and 'good', assumptions too deep-rooted to come under question, although the obvious question remains: 'good' for whom or what? I would argue, however, that what Lessing is demonstrating is the extent to which all *public* discourse – the discourse of power – presumes the primacy of reason and intellect as a basis for value-judgments. Such discourse validates knowledge of a specific kind – systematic, categorical and verifiable by 'scientific' experiment. In the private sphere to which women have traditionally been relegated, a different kind of discourse has held sway – dismissively categorized by male discourse as gossip, women's talk, even 'old wives' tales', embodying intuition, emotion, and an ability to distinguish the 'nice' and the 'good' without reference to officially sanctioned scales of assessment. Such discourse does not, however, enter in unmodified form into inter-sexual relationships, which are dominated by patriarchal discourse.

There is, Anna finds, a 'knowing' which cannot be put into words, since it exists outside the parameters of existing discourse, of existing representations of reality. She seems at times therefore to trust only non-verbal communication: a kiss can convey real feelings which words only cancel out (p. 333). *The Golden Notebook* is a very sensational novel, in the original sense of the word. Anxiety is experienced and described as a clenched stomach, nausea and physical illness, love not only as orgasm, but as the preparation of food. Physical sensation provides the key to Anna's state of mind. Her body becomes aware of the approaching end of a love affair long before her mind or her emotions can admit to such. When she touches a plant, she can feel either a 'kinship with the working roots, the breathing leaves', or a hostility emanating from the prisoner in the earthenware pot; at such times her curtains feel slippery and slimy, hanging 'like dead skin, or a lifeless corpse' (p. 571). To be happy, on the other hand, and sane, is for it to 'be a delight to feel the roughness of a carpet under smooth soles . . . If this goes, then the conviction of life goes too' (p. 591).

Nevertheless, Anna is a writer, committed to attempting to communicate what she 'knows', in particular this physical quality of life which she perceives as a central 'reality'. Throughout the text of *The Golden Notebook* she is engaged in a conflict between the language of desire and the language of reality. The language of desire is the language of the group, always prescriptive and characterized by rhetorical abstractions and phantom idealizations of what ought to be, such as we found in the reviews of *Frontiers of War*, in the discourse of the political group, and in the language of sexual identity. In contrast, the language of reality which she struggles to achieve is characterized by concrete reality, such as can be found in Anna's anecdotal writing – brief accounts of meetings and events which repeatedly expose the gaps and silences in the political discourse – and in her outlines of short stories, realizations of feelings and ideas which have arisen directly out of her personal experience, however unwelcome their implications. Like her dreams, such a discourse speaks symbolically, thus evading rigid definition and closure of meaning, while maintaining its grounding in direct, often physical, experience.

It is this same conflict of discourses which is ultimately seen to epitomize the warring relationship between art and politics. Anna eventually decides that art must be personal, the language of reality, as opposed to the impersonality of political discourse, which articulates the ideology of the party. While reviewing novels herself, she concludes that in all the banal writing sent to her the only flashes of genuine art arise out of a 'deep, suddenly stark, undisguisable private emotion'. In contrast, what is called by the party 'healthy' art is essentially impersonal: 'Its banality is that of impersonality' (p. 344). Art cannot, by definition, therefore be used for propaganda. This same art, moreover, this 'fiction', may, as was suggested above, be a repository of truth, in so far as 'truth' can be defined in terms of subjective experience. While Anna had tried unsuccessfully to capture the truth in the Blue Notebook, she finds that she had instead 'written the truth in the yellow diary' (p. 543) – the diary devoted to fiction. In fictional discourse she can write what cannot be admitted to her conscious self, what cannot be articulated in her 'realistic', autobiographical discourse, which only admits of certain aspects of the self. Through fiction as in dream can speak the repressed self, which the constructed, conforming self fails to acknowledge.

Anna therefore learns to accept her own fragmentation. The variety of discourses in which each individual is situated is indicative of the variety of roles each plays: 'Fascinating – the roles we play, the way we play parts' (p. 167). The subject acts out a role confident that others will recognize its significance and adopt the appropriate role in response, thus negating the need for individual response to an individual situation. But the jarring which occurs as subjects slip in and out of roles makes lasting relationships almost impossible, as each finds the other in the partnership increasingly elusive. This is the cause of the anxiety Anna feels with Saul, who can appear unpredictably in the role of the egocentric, yet intelligent and sensitive man, the loud-mouthed, self-proclaimed lone wolf, or the simple lecher. But the only way of being 'whole' is by blocking off that conflict which is an inevitable reality, by ignoring the split between the conforming and the repressed self. Among the parts of the Blue Notebook that she scores out is the statement: 'humanism stands for the whole person, the whole individual, striving to become as conscious and responsible as possible' (p. 354). Wholeness implies completion, a finite entity defined in terms of what it excludes, of what does not belong to the 'whole'. In contrast, fragmentation leads to formlessness, which precludes wholeness, though not unity, a point I shall return to later. As she tells Mother Sugar, 'the raw unfinished quality' of her life was 'precisely what was valuable in it' (p. 239).

Anna continues to attempt to hold together her feeling self and her intellect, which she feels threatened by her breakdown, feeling strongly that that intelligence is essential to her identity. But she ceases to attempt to *reconcile* them, to eliminate all contradictions, to create order and form. This personal attitude relates back to an earlier political insight: 'The battles and conflicts and debates inside our group . . . might have driven it into growth' (pp. 85–6) if it had not been for that dominant impulse to centralize, to impose conformity. The need for wholeness which drove her to join the party is now seen as a denial of the value of the discordant voice, which attempts to break through the smothering weight of ideology at the risk of incurring rejection and isolation. The experience of breakdown which she and her lover Saul undergo together suggests to her a positive alternative to wholeness. Her character Ella finds that her short stories all share 'patterns of defeat, death, irony', which she can nevertheless turn into 'victory', since the 'cracking up' which her characters undergo is an 'attempt to transcend their own limits' (p. 454). Rather than the closure and finality of 'wholeness', there is a value in openness and formlessness, which can lead to unity with what lies outside the self. As Anna writes in her own person, 'the fact they are cracked across, they're split, means they are keeping themselves open for something' (p. 460). The breakdown of barriers between Anna and Saul includes him in Anna's sense of self: 'I could no longer separate myself from Saul' (p. 567). Even on parting, she believes they 'would always be flesh of one flesh, and think each other's thoughts' (p. 617). Most significantly for her view of her writing, it is Saul's words which begin her new novel, ending her public silence. This act thus symbolically destroys the idea that fiction is one of the most privileged forms of self-expression, the product of the unique individual. When Anna accepts Saul's words – 'There are the two women you are, Anna. Write down: The two women were alone in the London flat' (p. 615) – she finally rejects the concept of subjectivity as unique, autonomous and unified, in favour of the notion of a decentred split self.

This changed view of the self clearly has important implications for Anna's view of her writing. When Tommy attempted suicide after reading her notebooks, she felt justified in her decision to stop writing for publication, since the consequences of sharing her sense of despair with others were evidently too great. However, it is Tommy himself who accuses Anna of limiting herself in those notebooks out of her fear of inner chaos. It was this same fear which had made her feel incapable of being a novelist in the truest sense of the word: she felt she lacked the 'intellectual or moral passion strong enough to create order'. But this desire for order was a conservative impulse, belied by her entire existence: the contents of her Notebooks constantly threaten to break through the boundaries she has attempted to impose on them. As Doris Lessing says of *The Golden Notebook* in her Preface, 'the essence of the book, the organization of it, everything in it, says implicitly and explicitly, that we must not divide things off, must not compartmentalize' (p. 10).

Anna therefore proposes to put all of herself into one book, the Golden Notebook. But it is an 'all' which remains split, contradictory, and open. It begins not with Anna's own words, but with Saul's inscription of a traditional children's rhyme – an assertion of authority undermined by the ironic use of children's language, a significant entry into the traditional domestic domain of women. Anna lets the 'dark' of the Black Notebook return, and for a time is 'sunk' in subjectivity and pain. But by bringing her intelligence into play she is also able to look at her past more directly than previously, and therefore to 'name' for *herself* what she fears, not letting her experience be appropriated into any other discourse. Through the 'projectionist' of her dreams, passing a beam of light into the darkness of her repressed self, Anna is able to review the script of her life in different versions which force her to look at it with a new emphasis. Her life, that is, is no more nor less than the shape and form which her memory gives to it – many shapes and many forms – not a single, fixed 'reality'.

Like the structure of *The Golden Notebook* itself, therefore, Anna succeeds in resisting the hierarchization of discourse which determines the relationship of centre to margin. The end of *The Golden Notebook* does not offer an 'answer', a solution for Anna or the reader. We are indeed left with two alternative endings: the Anna of the Golden Notebook returns to her writing, but the Anna of *Free Women* opts for the more directly practical, and political – teaching at night school, joining the Labour Party, and handing out advice to Dr North's patients. These alternative endings could be seen as appropriate outlets for Anna's repressed self and conforming self respectively, for both the Anna who attempts to find her own voice, and the Anna who attempts to find meaning in existing public discourse. It is tempting to see the conformist ending as the 'real' Anna's fictional construction, since *Free Women 5* is a recapitulation in summary of the preceding section of the Blue Notebook, demonstrating how the 'real life' material of the diaries is transformed into Anna's novel. According to this reading, Anna's 'third', her fictional ego-ideal, demonstrates what she feels she *ought* to do.

To interpret the relationship between *Free Women* and the Notebooks in this way, however, is to effect a reversal which has extraordinary implications. For the surface meaning of the text indicates Anna of *Free Women* to be the 'real life' author of the Notebooks, not a fictional projection. But the words which begin Anna's new novel are the words which begin *The Golden Notebook* itself. In spite of the surface structure of *The Golden Notebook*, the chronology of the different sections indicates that *Free Women* set in 1957, was written at a later date, after the Notebooks which are interwoven with it. What the reader had assumed to be an omniscient narrator's account of Anna's life, the 'reality' of the novel, is, it appears, Anna's own construction. There is therefore no 'conclusion' to *The Golden Notebook* because the end of the novel directs us immediately back to its beginning, making us feel that we need to re-read the whole novel differently in order to grasp its meaning. The status of novel and notebook is uncertain – the lines between fact and fiction are increasingly blurred. We are left with a chicken and egg situation, where it is no longer possible to locate with any certainty the originator of either the Notebooks or *Free Women*, since either could be the product of a fictive Anna, rather than any 'real' Anna. And since the author of *Free Women* is so elusive, it is equally difficult to determine the relationship of Doris Lessing to the narrator, to determine where or when the assumptions of the narrative command authorial assent. If there is no single originator of meaning, there can be no fixity of meaning, and no hierarchy of discourses – no privileging of one narrative 'voice' over another. There is a constant undercutting of the authority of any one voice or section of the text by another.

The text thus offers a model for the construction of the self by the self, rather than through ideology, since Anna is constantly engaged in writing and re-writing herself, refusing confinement and definition in a single, unified subject position. Whether writing of herself as 'I' or 'she', she refuses to make any single perspective central, thus ensuring that the text avoids creating its own margins, as it articulates those 'marginal' perspectives on 'reality' which I have suggested are *The Golden Notebook*'s dominant function.

In offering this reading of the novel, I am therefore only too aware of the danger of appearing to impose an authoritative, singular reading on it. This is not the same reading that I would have offered ten years ago, and in ten years time my view of it will no doubt have changed again. I have tried to stress that the strength and challenge of the novel is that it allows for – or rather demands – such plurality. It is an example of what Barthes calls a 'writerly' rather than 'readerly' text, in which the reader is actively engaged in constructing meaning rather than in passively consuming it. The novel's very title is, perhaps, a warning against the complacency of 'definitive' readings. If the reader is too ready to believe that Anna has found her final 'answer', once and for all, in her Golden Notebook, we should remember the myth of King Midas: the precious metal that is the goal of so many desires is also that which, as Midas found to his cost, solidifies, fixes and is death to all that lives. As Doris Lessing herself suggests, 'when a book's pattern and the shape of its inner life is as plain to the reader as it is to the author – then perhaps it is time to throw the book aside, as having had its day, and start again on something new' (Preface, p. 22).

4

Inner-Space Fiction: *Briefing for a Descent into Hell*

Briefing for a Descent into Hell is a puzzling and difficult novel, often neglected in critical accounts of Doris Lessing's work. The very nature of its subject-matter – the experience of a man diagnosed as suffering from mental breakdown – defies precise analysis. Yet it is an important novel, linking Lessing's earlier exploration of the construction of subjectivity in modern society with her later experiments in science-fiction. This 'inner-space fiction' is a synthesis, an exploration of subjectivity which leads the reader into new 'spaces', new imagined worlds, which offer an alien perspective on contemporary reality. The marginal perspective of the geographical colonies is replaced by that of the unconscious self which has been 'colonized' by the conscious, conforming self. And the marginal perspective of women is implicitly explored through a male subject whose own experience is marginalized by the label 'mental illness' on account of characteristics identifiable with those labelled 'female'.

The 'descent into hell' of the novel's title appears to refer to the mental condition of the patient, Charles Watkins, when admitted to hospital with amnesia, but it gradually emerges that the hell in question is in fact the 'real' world. When the patient's dream-self sleeps, it is 'dismal and alien', like 'entering a prison cell' (p. 62): it is at just these moments that the patient wakes in the hospital ward. Watkins's visionary experiences are intercut with his conversations with the doctors, and with letters and statements from his family and friends, all laying claim to some knowledge of Charles Watkins. The conflict between his subjective perceptions, and their perception of him is the novel's main concern, for it develops the idea presented in both *The Four-Gated City* and *The Golden Notebook* that mental breakdown is a potentially liberating and instructive experience, capable of contributing to the self-awareness and growth not only of the individual subject but of society as a whole. Mental hospitals are described as places where 'cracks' in individuals might let 'light . . . shine through at last' (p. 130). In mental illness the controls of 'sanity' are removed, leaving the unconscious free to speak. In his dreams in hospital, Watkins undertakes a mythical journey which presents a continual challenge to the nature and values of the 'real' world of the hospital.

Watkins's dream begins with a sea journey,[1] in which he is at once Jason, in pursuit of his 'purpose', and a second Odysseus fighting against the lure of the Sirens. He is a Sinbad, a Jonah, an Ancient Mariner left alone on board ship, a Judas, 'branded' as guilty when only his eleven companions ascend in the heavenly Crystal (p. 25). Because he is unable to remember the principle of Unity which should be his goal, he is fated to journey 'round and round'. The traveller is, however, rendered 'purged and salt-scoured and guiltless' (p. 60) by his journey, so that on reaching shore he enters a kind of Eden. Here is 'calm and plenty', 'paradise', where a man may lie down safely with the 'golden spotted beast' (p. 41). Even in an abandoned city, he feels among friends. Here too is re-enacted the Fall, and as in the Christian version, mankind's sin is revealed through the relationship of male and female, with the further implication that what is wrong with man is woman. While the traveller knows he ought to be preparing the city for the visit of the Crystal, so that he may be reunited with his fellow-travellers, restored to his higher purpose, he finds himself driven instead by the moon's circling, another variant on the cycle of forgetting from which he is trying to escape. He is 'moonstruck', 'moon-crazed', 'lunatic' (pp. 57, 59). His sudden consciousness of a smell of blood implicitly connects the moon's phases with the female menstrual cycle, underlining the traditional association between the moon, female sexuality, and insanity.

1. Some critics have commented on the obvious links between this novel and R.D. Laing's *The Politics of Experience* (Harmondsworth: Penguin, 1967), particularly as regards the 'sea voyage' of Laing's patient, Jesse Watkins. See, for example, Elaine Showalter, *The Female Malady: Women, Madness and English Culture 1830–1980* (London: Virago, 1987).
   Lessing herself, however, claims not to have read this book before writing her novel.

More explicitly, it is with women that the traveller becomes conscious of his carnality: with three blood-smeared women he eats flesh and dances over the body of a dead infant – significantly male. Now too he feels the need to cover himself. In contrast, he perceives his higher nature as that part of himself governed by 'the Sun, man's father and creator' (p. 57). While seeking entry to the Crystal, he is 'the sun's child', longing for the *'clean* sunlight' (p. 65, my italics), but he cannot resist the moon's forces because he is himself split, operating according to different laws, according to whether the moon (female) or sun (male) is dominant. When the traveller cannot see the Crystal, he feels he has failed dreadfully through his own fault. The consequences of his failure are graphically depicted in the subsequent arrival of the rat-dogs, their war with the apes, their self-destruction through violence and sexuality, and their pollution of land and sea. It is only when rescued by the white bird, 'watchful' and 'severe', a symbolic conscience, that the traveller is once more able to clean the city and enter the Crystal.

The journey can be seen as enacting in symbolic form different stages in the process of repression that accompanies socialization. The primal repression of the infant's desire for its mother, for re-entry to the womb, is evident in the traveller's sense of loss and exclusion from the Crystal or disc, accompanied by his intense sense of guilt. Because his desires are forbidden, they must be displaced onto another goal, and his original desire forgotten, forming the unconscious. The success with which the traveller achieves this displacement is suggested in his feeling guilt-free on reaching shore. This entry into a primitive civilization, to which the traveller feels he belongs, even though it appears to have been long abandoned, can be seen as representing entry into the symbolic order of language. The traveller evidently accepts that order and the values and categories inscribed in it, his desire being displaced onto a new goal – the cleaning of the city – which will earn him approval, and by which he may ultimately *merit* his displaced ideal of entry into the Crystal. His acceptance is evident too in the splitting of himself into the categories already provided by that order, into 'male' self and 'female' self. Furthermore, the ideological process is evident in the transference of his repressed guilt onto that self he labels female, so that all that is valued – his spiritual and intellectual aspirations and ideals – is attached to the male self, while what is deemed undesirable – his carnality – is attached to the 'female'. Through this process, a patriarchal society is enabled to *justify* repressing the gender it has constructed in these terms. If men fail to fulfil society's ideals, it is because they are frustrated by that animal nature for which woman, as mother and mate, is implicitly responsible. This dream-journey, therefore, is not simply a re-working of the patriarchal myth of the Fall, but a demonstration of the ideological process underlying such myths.

This Fall is, like so many others, 'fortunate': the traveller finally achieves understanding inside the Crystal. But this understanding hints at the possibility of transcending patriarchal ideology. When he recognizes that 'together [they] made a whole' (p. 91), that 'whole' includes not only his lost companions, but the women of the city now absorbed into his own mind (p. 89). Losing his sense of differentiation, which the symbolic order develops to a high degree, he acquires instead a sense of identity based on his similarity to others. But this myth of integration involves a form of regression to the pre-linguistic state, when the infant had no sense of the distinction between self and non-self. Entering the Disc is an obvious symbol of a return to the womb: it thus implies that this state cannot be achieved *within* the social order. The myth thus reinforces the idea that there is no way of being outside ideology, once the subject has acquired language and a place in the social order.

Watkins's dreams continue to enact the processes of repression, both psychological and institutional, in a variety of forms. The first stage in this process, the constitution of the subject – the separation of the 'I' from all that is not 'I' – is depicted in a vivid and moving account of birth and infancy. This follows a whimsical scene in which messengers from a superior intelligence are briefed for a journey to Earth, where they are to reawaken previous messengers and alert potentially responsive humans to their central purpose – the need to live in Harmony with the Laws of Existence. But a complete change of tone emphasizes the sense of tragic waste implicit in the concept of the infant messenger, with its superior capacity for growth, awareness and curiosity, for new life at every level. This episode gives dramatic expression to the Wordsworthian concept that 'our birth is but a sleep and a forgetting', as the infant loses its sense of unity with what lies outside it, which becomes identified instead as the obstacle to its desires. Dependent on its parents for the satisfaction of its most fundamental physical needs, its intense thirst for new experience, its 'hell of want' (p. 126), is displaced by its desire for parental approval. That approval is, in turn, dependent on the infant's conformity to the ideal of infant goodness which in this culture is defined as total passivity. The 'good' baby is the sleeping baby: 'I sleep so that they love me' (p. 128). So effectively is this desire for sleep constructed in the infant that it becomes a focus of adult longing – the elderly, the unhappy everywhere demand, 'give me what you trained me to need' (p. 129). Moreover, since the infant's original desires have been repressed into the unconscious, in sleep these desires manifest themselves, offering in dreams images of the self at once threatening to the conforming self and the object of intense, though repressed longing. Sleep is therefore doubly to be desired.

The novel also mounts a forceful attack on those cultural institutions which are generally regarded as society's strength, embodying and furthering its highest aspirations and ideals. In his 'real' life, Charles Watkins is a Professor of Classics, married, with two children. He is very much a functioning member of the cultural Establishment, and equally well placed to be aware of any of its flaws. His growing perception of the limitations of these institutions, used to justify the dominant ideology and to repress all forms of thought which threaten its security, is suggested in the retrospective narrative of the events leading to his breakdown. Rosemary Baines, a teacher, is deeply roused by a public lecture the Professor delivered during that period. His lecture on education makes her feel 'slapped out of a daydream' (p. 147), so that she remembers things she had forgotten when 'the prison shades' (p. 158) came down. She recalls his argument that education is a vital bridge between past, present and future, which can and should challenge existing ideological structures. He suggested that all adults, conscious of their own failures, see children as beings 'who could grow up into a race altogether superior to ourselves': education is therefore always seen as a potential means of fulfilling that dream. Such a dream, however, is doomed to defeat by that process of repression so vividly depicted in the birth sequence. Whatever lip-service is paid to the ideal of education, that ideal depends on keeping curiosity alive, which represents too great a threat to the dominant ideology and demands too much from adults enervated by the sleep-culture. Children instead become 'prisoners': in each infant 'individuality is covered over by what the parents say he is' (p. 151), constructing their child's identity according to ideological norms.

Another, though less direct, witness to the Professor's work shows symptoms similar to Charles's own, associated with a disquiet about his discipline, archaeology, which echoes Watkins's feelings about his. Rosemary's friend, Frederick Larson, also experiences a sudden sense of 'extra wakefulness': 'It was as if I approached a mirror and found it blank' (p. 161). That is, instead of accepting as his identity the mirror image reflected by society, validating or censoring his desires, he becomes again a *tabula rasa*. But this loss of a preconstructed and defined subject position, his sense of what constitutes 'I', results in the stammering which also afflicts Watkins. And while lecturing, he becomes conscious of a stream of thought parallel to his usual logical discourse – a stream his conforming self dismisses as 'cranky', but in which his repressed self surfaces. This 'problem' is however cured by sedatives, and by a self-imposed form of censorship, which involves bringing to consciousness and reviewing every word before it is enunciated. The subject's complicity in the maintenance of an ideology that oppresses even itself is nowhere suggested more vividly.

Like Larson, Watkins succeeds in controlling his stammer – and all that it implies – because raising to consciousness his full sense of what is wrong with society would destroy his own sense of identity, as his subsequent amnesia proves. It is only in the dreams which follow that he can be fully explicit. In one of his more sober 'visions', delivered in a lecturing, analytic tone appropriate to his professional life, Watkins castigates professions such as his own. He sees their very confidence and authority as guarantees that any challenge to their stranglehold over ways of seeing will be stifled. Their arrogant faith in 'progress' prevents them from learning from the lessons of the past: authoritative statements about 'truth' go on being made in spite of the all too obvious fallibility of every generation. Blinkered, moreover, by the assumptions of their own ideology, Western historians and archaeologists can only evaluate other cultures in modern terms: societies living in perfect harmony with their surroundings must nevertheless be 'primitive' because undeveloped technologically. Obsessed with facts and things themselves, twentieth-century analysts can only judge other civilizations on the basis of *their* surviving artefacts, which – as Larson's later parody directed at twentieth-century society shows (pp. 158–9) – does scant justice to any civilization.

To dismiss the views of any of these characters as 'crankiness', the 'loony left' or even symptoms of mental illness is, therefore, to miss the point. For the novel suggests that only such disjunctions of the 'normal' can create sufficient detachment from the dominant ideology to make possible a radical critique of that ideology. Watkins's mythical dream journey disrupts the symbolic order which usually censors his consciousness of repression. Anxiety is thus a message from 'that other part of ourselves' (p. 247), the repressed, questioning self, warning of the urgent need for change. Medical treatment in the form of drugs, hospitalization and even shock therapy may be necessary with extreme cases of such 'disturbance', but for most the ideological apparatus operates with far more subtle but equally powerful effect.

For the main conflict enacted by the novel is not simply one between doctor and patient, but between different discourses – different linguistic practices which embody different ways of seeing, of structuring reality. The discourse adopted by Charles's doctors derives its validity from observable facts, from its so-called objectivity. The 'Admittance Sheet' with which the novel opens is an extreme, but representative example. The lack of 'marks of identity' on the patient limit the observations that can be made, but the desire to label this Unknown dominates the professional response. This attempt at definitive identification is, of course, characteristic of the scientific discipline in which the doctors have been trained. In her 'Afterword' to this novel, Lessing criticizes an education system which is devoted to teaching children 'how to use labels' and 'define' (p. 252), in the mistaken belief that such labelling is equivalent to knowledge or understanding. Indeed, from the cosmic view of the Briefing, science is this society's 'most recent religion', distinguished, like its predecessors, by its tendency to compartmentalize even while paying lip-service to the unity of life. Its discourse therefore has a dominant role.

Moreover, this categorical, classifying discourse is seen to be based on distinctions and categories which are not objective as claimed, but ultimately ideological. Examples of such have already been considered – the categorization of non-technological societies as 'primitive', the privileging of the 'rational' over the 'irrational' which empowers certificated medical experts to certify others as 'insane' or 'sick': it can only be 'irrational' to question the 'rationale' on which the social order is founded. The most fundamental assumption is that 'scientific', observable knowledge constitutes an ultimate reality, a higher 'truth' than any other. In this novel Lessing suggests, like more recent feminist theorists, that this kind of theoretical discourse, with its emphasis on distinguishing characteristics, classes, orders and hierarchies, embodies an inherently oppressive impulse to imprison reality in rigid structures.[2] In such systems, 'otherness', what does not fit, is suppressed or dismissed by such formulae as 'the exception that proves the rule', in order to preserve the consistency of the theory, its guarantee of authority.[3]

2. I am indebted for much of my argument relating to linguistic theory to Deborah Cameron, *Feminism and Linguistic Theory* (London: Macmillan, 1985).
3. Women are, in a patriarchal system, inevitably 'Other', as was argued by Simone de Beauvoir in *The Second Sex* (Harmondsworth: Penguin, 1984), an argument developed by the more recent theorist Luce Irigaray. See Moi, *Sexual/Textual Politics*, pp. 127–35.

Charles's discourse is clearly 'other', exploiting as it does all the poetic potential of language. Through word play and sound association he can experience three different meanings of a single syllable of sound in rapid succession – 'an eye indeed. Aye Aye. I. I could . . .' (p. 12). This enables him to move easily between different orders of reality, between the 'sea-bed' and the hospital bed. Rosemary Baines, in a letter describing her meeting with Charles shortly before his amnesia, recalls that then too his words – although odd by conventional standards – possessed their own logic, as 'if the sound, and not the meaning, of a word or syllable . . . gave birth to the next sentence or word' (p. 200). She suggests the relationship between sound and meaning has been seriously neglected. Although traditionally exploited by poets, non-referential forms of language are not generally regarded as having any 'meaning' that is relevant to 'real' life: these are marginalized discourses, appropriate only for poets and other madmen.

This poetic discourse gives voice to Charles's repressed, nonconforming self, freed to speak through the temporary silencing of his conforming social identity by amnesia. When the doctors assert that he is not a wandering sailor, that other self responds with the challenge, 'Then why do I think I'm one' (p. 29), asserting its own validity. The very different conditions governing this second self are evident throughout the dream journey. The traveller wishes to meet the inhabitants of the Crystal because 'they'll know [his] needs and there'll be no need to tell Them' (p. 18). That is, his needs and desires will create their own means of satisfaction, in contrast to the real world in which desire itself is the product of an ideological discourse. Similarly, when the traveller perceives in this Eden the foundations of a great house previously unnoticed, 'it was as if the knowledge of what [he] would see caused [him] to see' (p. 50). The constructing function of perception is here openly acknowledged – 'reality' is not already there, but dependent on what the subject believes to be there. The way is therefore opened for a reality that is the product of subjectivity, rather than ideologically structured.

But because the doctors do not share Charles's discourse, they cannot understand his subjective reality which is of a totally different order from theirs. At the very moment they assert their patient has 'less grip on reality', the text describes what the white bird of *truth* has revealed to the traveller. Although determined to 'find out more about' him (p. 17), they refuse to take any account of his view of himself. The patient is described as 'under the impression' – implicitly mistaken – that 'he is on some sort of voyage' (p. 11). While there is clearly a legitimate difficulty in reconciling this view with the patient's presence in the hospital bed, the doctors' insistence on the exclusive 'reality' of what can be immediately verified by the senses puts a barrier in the way of understanding their patient. They prefer to construct an identity for him on the basis of the reality they share, but which he does not recognize.

Moreover, in this conflict of discourses, there is an imbalance of power. The discourse employed by the doctors is also characterized by a literal-mindedness that is inherently oppressive. As the goddess Minna says in rebuke to Merk, during the Briefing, to be 'so literal-minded' is to be 'like them' (p. 113): to be literal-minded is to perceive and accept only a single meaning in any utterance. The two doctors ask Charles to 'talk more clearly' but forget that words are only symbols, signifiers which may have more than one signified. Neither is prepared to admit that his reading of the signs – linguistic or otherwise – may be wrong. While their own science of psychology theoretically recognizes the value of dream and myth, making use of such terms as 'Oedipus complex', neither registers the significance of Charles's use of names like Jason or Jonah, because these fall outside the descriptions of psychological conditions codified and accredited by their profession. While prepared to accept that his discourse may shed some light on his inner state, they are not ready to acknowledge that it might throw any light on their world. The power invested in their discourse is made brutally clear when they tell Charles, unequivocally and unhesitatingly, who he is, according to official documents: they state, 'you have no choice, Professor. We know that's who you are' (p. 140). The discourse that assumes privileged authority for itself is always suspect. They have the authority to make him remember what they '*know* to be true about him' (p. 143). Searching for single, authoritative meaning, their discourse asserts one kind of knowledge, one reality.

When the police and the doctors describe Charles, therefore, as 'rambling' (p. 11), they are criticizing his failure to use logical speech patterns which correspond to literal fact. It is ironic that they should use a metaphor to do so, since they characteristically limit this too to a single meaning: for them 'rambling' is a dead metaphor which has lost its original significance. They do not register the appropriateness of the word to Charles's inner life – his dream journey. Being unaware of the polysemic potential of their own words, then they will inevitably fail to understand Charles's discourse. Those like Charles Watkins who suggest that words and utterances may have more than one meaning are resisting the 'authorized version', rejecting the authority that legitimizes that version, and are therefore inherently subversive.

The choice of discourses dictated by the doctors is not only false but unnecessary. Quoting T.S. Eliot, Charles acknowledges that language is a limited though unavoidable means of communication: 'I gotta use words when I talk to you' (p. 105). Words can, however, be combined in a rich variety of discourses, different means of encoding or structuring the phenomena encountered by the human subject. Not only the myths and parables of the past are metaphoric, but modern scientific discourse itself, using terms like 'wavelength' and 'forcefield', and constructing models as means of explanation. Language is, after all, a symbolic system. As epigraphs to the novel, Doris Lessing uses quotations separated by 600 years:

> If yonder raindrop should its heart disclose,
> Behold therein a hundred seas displayed.
> In every atom, if thou gaze aright,
> Thousands of reasoning beings are contained . . .

> . . . this miniscule world of the sand grains is also the world of inconceivably minute beings, which swim through the liquid film around the grain of sand as fish would swim through the ocean covering the sphere of the earth . . .

The first is an example of poetic discourse, the second of the discourse of popular science, but both embody similar insights into the existence of worlds inaccessible to the naked eye. Charles's dreams develop this idea, demonstrating that similar concepts or events can be represented in different forms, each embodying a very different set of values. The Fall, for instance, is explained by the gods of the Briefing in terms of 'eating the fruit' or 'stealing the fire', equally effective metaphors for explaining that 'Knowledge brings a penalty' (p. 112). When one single mode of representation is privileged above all others, however, it becomes a dominant ideology, used as a form of social control. It becomes a means of internalizing the ethical system deemed to reinforce most effectively the existing power structure. Instead, the novel suggests, we need to understand many discourses, other perceptions of what might indeed be shared experience.

In keeping with this principle, the novel uses a variety of discourses to construct myths which demonstrate, rather than conceal, the operation of ideology, as I suggested in my discussion of Charles's first dream. The key events of the novel can be interpreted on a number of different levels: the 'realistic' surface account situates Charles's dreams in the context of a mental breakdown and thus renders them open to interpretation as drug-induced hallucinations; a psychoanalytic analysis retains the structure of the breakdown, but interprets the dreams more positively, as significant manifestations of the unconscious; seen in relation to the mythical central Briefing, his amnesia can be interpreted as a remembering – Charles forgets the identity he has assumed for his earthly mission because he has remembered his 'Message', which is that humanity must keep the laws of Harmony and Unity. Resisting the emphasis on individualism resulting from his or her social conditioning, each person must recognize their place in the whole. But in Earth's poisonous and polluted atmosphere all are in danger of forgetting this purpose, for 'it was part of this little organism's condition to discover and forget and discover and forget' (p. 99).

The more 'realistic' account renders this briefing as a war-time mission undertaken by Watkins, a more plausible version of a formative episode in his life. His account of his work with Yugoslav partisans during World War II is one of the most accessible episodes in the novel, in so far as it relates to events which we recognize as historically true, and is presented within a familiar realist narrative form. But this very familiarity should alert the reader to the element of codification. For this is a heroic adventure story in the Hemingway tradition: there is the idealization of the man of action and wartime comradeship, together with a love affair with a young female partisan, whose activities make her temporarily 'one of the boys', but whose tragic death prevents her abandonment of traditional femininity from posing a problem in 'everyday', post-war reality. In fact, this is yet another, more modern myth, taking place in a new Eden – 'The world as it was before man filled and fouled it' (p. 211). The partisans are inspired by the ideals represented by the 'Red Star', an ideal of unity echoing the message of the Crystal. Its potency is evident in the comrades' feeling that 'it was as if [they] remembered it' (p. 213), another hint of a prelapsarian state latent in the collective memory. Post-war history inevitably throws an ironic light on this particular political myth, endowing it with a strong sense of Romanticism. Such statements as 'It is only in love and in war that we escape from the sleep of necessity' (p. 210) *are* merely escapist: the rest of the novel suggests both love and war are means of evading the urgent need for global harmony.

The objective reality of this event thus becomes increasingly suspect, until it finally emerges that it never took place – at least not for Watkins, who appears to have 'borrowed' it from Miles Bovey. The validity of the episode rests not in any 'objective' reality it lays claim to, but in its metaphoric significance as an indicator of Charles's subjective experience. This is evident from its close correspondence with other formulations of that experience. The mission, like Charles's dream sea-journey, initially involves twelve men, but in both Charles is left alone. Konstantina, the partisan, is clearly both Conchita, left behind on the sea-shore, and Charles's 'real-life' mistress Constance. Both Edens are shattered by the spilling of blood, although Konstantina's death has a sacrificial function: she dies to protect her lover from a female deer in turn protecting her newly born kid, a paradigmatic condensation of the sexual and the maternal, the threat and salvation ascribed to the female. The sexual threat is thus erased from this Eden, obviating the need for further purgation and suffering on the hero's part. Parallels between the briefing which introduces this episode and its mythological counterpart also abound: in each case the 'messenger' is to be dropped into total darkness to seek out others with the same purpose. To describe the war-time mission as another myth is by no means, therefore, to undermine its significance or 'truth'.

The uncertain status and 'reality' of different parts of the narrative is partly, of course, due to the lack of explicit authorial guidance. Even at the end of the novel, where an impersonal third-person observer describes Charles's hospital friendship with his young fellow-patient Violet,[4] and his return to 'normality' after electric shock treatment, the reader works alone, for even this narrative voice is not omniscient, nor possessed of any authoritative, superior wisdom. The characters are depicted in a specific historical and geographical location, which carries special weight in the novel since it recognizably belongs to the 'real' world of the modern Western reader. But this reality in no way dominates the other versions of reality presented by the novel: their effect is to draw the reader's attention to the means by which this particular view of reality is embodied in the discourse of Realism – both literary and philosophical – and privileged by our culture. Charles's visionary experiences, in other words, exist to counter a reality that is unchallenged by self-consciousness.

No discourse in this novel, therefore, is privileged by its correspondence with the 'real world' of the reader, or through authorial narrative comment. Nor, on the other hand, can Charles's dream-life be said to be endowed with the traditional status of 'special pleading', the authority of the authentic, 'this is how I felt' witness. For instead of his

---

4. Violet's manner of dress – half Victorian young lady, half sexually provocative – enacts very clearly the Lacanian split between conforming and non-conforming selves.

experiences being presented consistently in the first person, they are presented through a series of narrative perspectives which break down any sense of a pre-existent, unified subject, so that there can be no coherent, identifiable originator of meaning. No validity derives from the authority of the perceiving subject, only from the form of the perception itself: the text's 'conviction' resides in its language. The richly polysemic poetic discourse of Watkins's inner life, a voice speaking from the margins of 'insanity', makes its own implicit comment on the sterile, univocal discourse of the doctors. When words have more than one meaning, and none is more 'basic' than another, the union of signifier and signified in a word, which sign-systems tend to solidify, breaks down. The signifier becomes 'free-floating': the image therefore retains its potential *as* image, liberated to 'mean' many things, and freed from its usual associations in such a way that its reality as word, sound, object in itself, is more strongly felt, as Rosemary Baines feels it in Charles's discourse.

The contrast drawn here anticipates Julia Kristeva's distinction between 'semiotic' and 'symbolic' texts. According to Kristeva, with entry to the symbolic order of language, the influence of the *chora*, the pre-Oedipal phase in which mother and infant enjoy perfect unity, is repressed. But this influence can manifest itself indirectly through rhythm, intonation, and textual disruption, all aspects of language which the discourses of madness and poetry draw on, as does the discourse of Charles's 'sickness'.[5] The sea on which Watkins begins his journey is a symbol of those bodily and unconscious rhythms which constantly disrupt the rigid chronological and spatial order into which the doctors attempt to insert him. The complex mythic layers of his inner life reveal the poverty of the doctors' literal-minded attempts to construct him as a text which illustrates their own hypothesis. Given that the symbolic order is inscribed with the values of the dominant patriarchal order, what is repressed with the semiotic is what that order constructs as 'female' – all that is undesirable or unnecessary to the maintenance of power and therefore marginalized in the process of gender differentiation, illustrated in this novel's version of the Fall.

Briefing for a Descent into Hell passes, therefore, an implicit judgement on all systems that derive power from a tyrannical insistence on authoritative single meanings, determined by the system itself. Those whom such systems marginalize are rendered powerless if they accept its definitions of themselves. Before his 'awakening', Watkins in

5. See Moi, *Sexual/Textual Politics*, pp. 153–63.

his letters uses what Deborah Cameron calls 'idle discourse', a discourse which reproduces these power relations as given and natural. This impoverished discourse takes meaning and definition for granted as closed and final. In contrast, the discourse of Charles's awakened repressed self, in emphasizing the plurality of meaning, draws attention to those practices by which idle discourse is constructed and encouraged. In this respect it is, as I have already suggested, subversive, typical of 'radical' discourse, as defined by feminists like Cameron. And it is thus – through a male protagonist – that Lessing projects that 'marginal' feminist view which I have suggested characterizes her fiction. She is, however, more pessimistic about the power of such a challenge than more recent theorists. As Postscript to the novel, she includes the following 'small relevant reminiscence' about an idea for a film: 'The point of this film was that the hero's or protagonist's extra sensitivity and perception must be a handicap in a society organized as ours is, to favour the conforming, the average, the obedient' (p. 251).

5

Canopus in Argos: Archives

(i) Structuralist Fiction

> The role of a properly structuralist imagination will of necessity be futuristic.[1]

In his discussion of the 'structuralist imagination', Robert Scholes argues that, as a philosophy, structuralism constitutes a reaction to existential Marxism: in contrast to an 'attractive vision of a future in which all men are free, equal and fulfilled human beings', in which humanity is 'moving towards a progressive future in a progressive way', structuralism assumes that 'man is in a system not necessarily arranged for his benefit' (p. 193). Doris Lessing has expressed her own scepticism about the concept of progress in terms very similar to Scholes: 'That everything is for the best, justice will prevail, that human beings are equal, that if we try hard enough, society is going to become perfect . . . These are attitudes that seem increasingly absurd'.[2] I have therefore used the term 'structuralist fiction' to describe the novel-sequence in which that scepticism finds its clearest expression. In *Canopus in Argos* it finds appropriate expression in the tradition of science or space fiction, of which Lessing writes: 'These dazzlers have mapped our world, or worlds for us, have told us what is going on and in ways no one else has done, have described our nasty present long ago, when it was still the future and the official scientific spokesmen were saying that all manner of things now happening were

1. Robert Scholes, *Structuralism in Literature: An Introduction* (Yale University Press, 1974), p. 200.
2. Interview with Robert Rubens, *Queen*, 21 August 1962, p. 31.

impossible.'[3] By creating make-believe worlds which develop techno-logical and scientific speculation beyond the immediately possible, but based on what is known, the writer can articulate fears for the future of the world at the same time as exploring alternative models of social organization.

Lessing's work has always, I have suggested, demonstrated the limits of realism – the difficulties of exploring alternative modes of experi-ence and perception in a form inscribed with the values of Western humanism. To achieve critical distance from that ideology, her novels adopt what I have called 'marginal' narrative perspectives. But the growing influence of those values throughout the world appears to have increased her pessimism about the future to the extent that such a 'margin' can now only be found outside the planet itself, in the view-point of other planets in the galaxy. While the construction of a fic-tional planetary system thus makes possible a logical development of Lessing's earlier colonial perspective, it also, however, introduces a radical change: humanity is not at the centre of this system, for Earth, under the name of Shikasta, is a mere colony. Rather than viewing the 'centre' from the margins, we are now asked to see the centre of our existence as itself 'marginal'.

But if this sequence is the most experimental of Lessing's fictions, measured in terms of its distance from realism, it is paradoxically also the most traditional. She points out that many science-fiction writers have 'explored the sacred literatures of the world', acknowledging that *Shikasta* itself takes the Old Testament as its 'starting-point'. Lessing claims, moreover, that the 'sacred literatures of all races and nations have many things in common' (I,10), a pool of mythic narratives and figures used to explain creation, evolution and humanity's place in the universe. This implies a concern with constants of human behaviour and thought, whereas science-fiction is more often concerned with the particular features of contemporary society. The cosmology of *Shikasta* and *The Sirian Experiments* thus provides a new mythology: a galactic conflict used to account for the shifting fortunes of Earth history.

Other novels in the sequence are more appropriately termed 'fables', teaching stories comparable with those of the Sufis or New Testament parables. The sequence as a whole is a parable for our self-improvement, designed to outwit what Nancy Hardin calls the 'Old

3. Introduction to *Shikasta*, p. 9. All further references to the *Canopus* sequence will follow the relevant quotation in the text. I have included Volume numbers to avoid confusion.

Villain' – 'the patterns of conditioned thinking which form the prison in which we all live'.[4] Like the earlier fiction, these novels explore the construction of these 'patterns', the process by which certain ways of seeing become dominant. Like Canopean students, the reader is required to try out 'different focuses' (I,16) for reviewing Shikastan history. For a change of perspective may lead to a change in understanding. 'History' is inseparable from historiography, what is remembered being dependent on *who* is remembering and *when*. Each new experience changes our perception of the past, so that our life histories are constantly being modified as each new life event offers the possibility of a new ending. Lessing's 'Archives', therefore, offer the reader a variety of new angles from which to view the patterns of human history and thought.

I have chosen for more detailed analysis Volumes I and IV of the sequence – *Shikasta* and *The Making of the Representative for Planet 8*, two novels which exemplify the extremes of perspective offered by the sequence. *Shikasta* establishes the cosmic framework of the sequence, and its system of values. The novel re-writes the history of the Earth up to and beyond the Third World War which Doris Lessing sees as inevitable. Written from the perspective of a species of superior beings, inhabitants of Canopus, it presents Western civilization in particular in the less than flattering perspective of other cultures. Its mix of fable, futuristic fantasy, and pseudo-documentary accounts of twentieth-century Earth history enables the reader to maintain some contact with the familiar world of contemporary reality while becoming familiar with Lessing's imaginary construction. In the rest of the sequence, the existence of the 'real' world is implicit rather than explicit, to be measured against the fictional construct. *The Making of the Representative for Planet 8* operates at the opposite end of the spectrum, in that it examines closely the fate of a single planet at a particular moment in its history, from the point of view of an inhabitant of that planet. A brief discussion of the final volume – *The Sentimental Agents in the Volyen Empire* – will, in conclusion, show how its exploration of discourse and ideology illuminates the sequence as a whole.

Note on the Canopean Empire

Doris Lessing has taken the names of Sirius and Canopus, the two brightest stars in the constellation Argo Navis, for the rival Empires in

4. Hardin, 'Doris Lessing', p. 151.

her Argos galaxy. Her mythology is so constructed as to account both for specific moments in Earth history and for the eternal conflict of good and evil. After initial conflict, Canopus and Sirius agree to avoid interfering with each other's interests in lesser planets. They both remain, however, sworn enemies of the evil Puttioran Empire, based on the evil planet Shammat – the father of lies, of sham – which is equally determined to exercise *its* influence. Canopus's influence is presented as the most benign, because its primary concern is not self-interest but observing the Necessity – the need to live in harmony with the cosmic order. Sirius, though well-intentioned, suffers from internal division as to its true purpose. The colonized planets are usually referred to only by number, the exception being Rohanda, 'the fruit-ful', representing Earth. Canopus becomes interested in this planet, as a possible home for the inhabitants of the doomed Planet 8, after a burst of radiation produces a rapidly evolving species full of variety and potential. Canopus therefore introduces volunteers from Planet 10 to boost this evolutionary process, establishing in the 'Time of the Giants' a Lock between itself and Rohanda which ensures a beneficial flow of influence. Its plans are, however, halted by the Catastrophe, a realignment of the stars – a dis-aster – which breaks the lock and initiates the process of degeneration which we know as Earth history. Rohanda is accordingly renamed Shikasta, 'the hurt, the damaged' (I,38).

(ii) 'Shikasta'

Canopean agents enter Shikasta through the dangerous Zone 6. Together with ordinary human souls, they wait for a suitable incarna-tion in a place dominated by 'nostalgia', the same emotion that proved such a trap for Martha Quest. The entry itself is depicted in terms reminiscent of the birth sequence in *Briefing for a Descent into Hell*: the agent Johor describes how their 'minds, [their] beings, were alert and knowing, but [their] memories had already slid away, dissolved' (I,265), evoking the same state of awareness described in the infant entering into a new identity. Charles Watkins's story could indeed be incorporated into *Shikasta*, alongside the histories of agents sent to Shikasta/Earth after World War II, without appearing in any way out of place. Lynda Coldridge, whose story plays an important part in *The Four-Gated City*, actually reappears in this sequence, to exemplify the paranormal powers depicted in the earlier novel. Nevertheless, in spite of such links with Lessing's earlier work, the reader embarking on *Shikasta* is likely to be more conscious of differences: instead of beginning with an individual human experience, taking place in a world recognizably our own, this novel confronts us with an alien universe, and a disconcertingly remote narrator.

The author warns us of the need to reorientate ourselves from the outset. The text introduces itself as a kind of anti-novel, a set of archives purporting to be instructional rather than entertaining. This claim is reinforced by the presence of footnotes, cross-references, historical summaries, additional notes and bibliographies. All these are at the forefront of the novel, preceding any engagement with smaller-scale narratives, rather than simply being used to authenticate them. A reversal takes place whereby those stories of human behaviour which are most familiar and accessible to the real reader are presented as illustration of conduct too extreme for the comprehension of the implied reader – the Canopean student. The reader's perspective is thus wrenched into an unfamiliar alignment with another, by which our own world and its assumptions are made to appear not only lacking but incomprehensible. This onslaught on 'the Old Villain' is underlined by the dominant narrative voice. Johor, a Canopean agent whose name carries echoes of the Hebrew term for God, Jahweh, offers none of the 'special pleading' that we associate with first-person narrators. Although claiming to have become subject to emotionalism under the influence of the Shikastan atmosphere, he shows no obvious subjective bias, and seems to have little interest in the usual concerns of the individual. Androgynous, endowed with no individualizing background, habits or tastes, and using a language free from colloquialisms or other personal stylistic markers, he is in the main too disembodied, too removed from the world and assumptions of the reader, to act as an ideal reader, a focal point for his or her concerns.

This 'anti-novel' element is further evident in the novel's characterization, particularly in its first half. The emphasis is less on individuality or psychological realism than on the behaviour of social groups, races, or species. Interest focuses on situation rather than character, as it traditionally does in myth and fable. In his reports on those individuals whom the renegade Canopean agent Taufiq failed to contact, Johor provides potted biographies containing details of family and social context such as we might expect to find in an author's notes for a conventional novel. But these notes are never 'fleshed out', since their function is to illustrate typical patterns of behaviour. When individual differences are so played down, the role of social and ideological structuring emerges much more sharply.

Only when these 'types' are given voices do they take on some semblance of individual characterization, as is the case with the diaries of Rachel Sherban. Rachel and her brother Ben are among the Shikastans regarded by Canopus as promising genetic material. Having visited Shikasta in previous lives, which they wasted in 'self-indulgence and weakness . . . and forgetfulness' (I,21), both now have another chance to learn from those earlier visits and to break free from the deadly cycle of purposeless, egotistical existence, so as not to be forced to repeat the process of incarnation. Rachel's highly personal and confused feelings about her brother George, the latest incarnation of Johor, hinder her understanding of his capacities, activities and motives. By Canopean standards those feelings are petty and partial, but they provide a point of anchorage for the reader, embodying an earth-bound perspective. Rachel herself, however, gradually senses the limitations of this perspective: she initially judges her Moroccan neighbours, Naseem and Shireen, in the 'western way' (I,297), according to standards which highlight their poverty, their harsh and primitive life-style, and the repression of the woman. With time and shared experience, however, she learns to appreciate and even envy their 'mystery' (I,298), their obvious joy and sense of communion. The process of learning which Rachel undergoes in the course of her own narrative is shared by the reader, who is thus asked to consider the limitations of his or her own perspective.

The narrative method of the novel suggests, therefore, how *not* to read the text – not to focus on personal, subjective motivation and individualistic psychology. In contrast, the implication of realist fiction is that only by involving the reader directly in the thoughts and feelings of highly individualized characters in specific situations can the reader be made to understand and feel for that individual. Even if that individual's experience is intended to be representative, it is conventionally understood that the situation of a group or class is best understood through the individual case, where the individual is representative of the group, as is true of Lessing's early fiction, more closely related to the realist tradition. It is assumed that no reader can be expected to feel concern for an anonymous mass, that no one can weep for the unknown soldier. *Canopus in Argos* challenges this view and indeed shifts the focus of the fiction away from emotional identification to intellectual perception, to changing the bases of our judgement.

For the history of Shikasta is used to demonstrate where the obsession with individuality can lead, if a society becomes so egocentric that it loses its concern for the survival of the race, or species – the primary evolutionary imperative. In cosmic terms this degeneration is explained as the result of the reduction of SOWF – 'substance-of-we-feeling' – reaching the planet from Canopus after the Catastrophe (I,97). As Johor puts it, 'To identify with ourselves as individuals – this is the very essence of the Degenerative Disease' (I,55). If unable to see itself as a whole, the human race is doomed to self-destruction.

The belief in individuality is, moreover, shown to be based on spurious ideas of 'difference' which are simply ideological constructs without real foundation. The narrator describes how during World War II the 'two great Dictatorships [Hitler and Stalin] . . . spread ideologies based on the suppression and oppression of whole populations of differing sects' (I,112). From the Canopean point of view these warring nations thus appear identical. Even those opposed to them are in the 'toils of one of the ideologies', acting 'always in the name of the masses' (I,113), whom they are doomed to betray because of their ideological blinkers. The dissenting young, for example, are so convinced that they alone are 'in the right' (I,178) that they too get caught up in the inevitable process whereby each new 'centre' creates its own margins, every group splits into factions. The sense of difference, the 'cocoon of righteousness', precludes any awareness of what unites them all. Thus the nations of Shikasta prepare to destroy or enslave each other – 'in the name of progress, and equality and development and democracy' (I,120). Only the technocrats are united, agreed in their analysis of the planet's perilous condition.

In its analysis of the twentieth century, the 'age of ideology' as it is known in Canopean history books, *Shikasta* thus mounts a powerful attack on those 'patterns', ideological structures, through which subjects acquire that illusory 'individuality', that sense of being an autonomous, unified subject, at the price of self-division and repression. The Canopean agent, Taufiq, for instance, in his 1950s incarnation as John Brent-Oxford, a British lawyer, falls prey to 'one of the strongest of the false ideas of that epoch, politics' (I,100). The 'suppressed inner qualities' (I,103) of 'his deepest self' (I,108) are sacrificed to the imaginary self constructed by the ideals of left-wing politics. It is only when his 'other self' speaks to him through the voice of Johor, as in a dream, that these 'alternative ways of thought' can overthrow the patterns imposed by his 'rational self' (I,105), resulting in the kind of mental breakdown so often presented by Lessing as a source of hope. Those Shikastans who show potential in Canopean terms are also described as 'divided', as feeling at war with themselves. A Worker's Leader symptomatically puts himself on trial to try to demonstrate his sense of treachery. Much of the growing discontent on the planet derives from these dissatisfied 'real selves . . . hidden selves' (I,120). Politics, it is suggested, is both the most powerful and the most dangerous of ideologies because it is inherently divisive: political thought is marked by its 'crippling partiality' (I,101). To be political is to take sides, to adopt a point of view, of which the subject then becomes a prisoner.

For ideology suppresses self-doubt. Nationalism, for instance, generates not only a sense of difference but a sense of superiority which justifies the oppression of other nations, and races. Or rather, to use the discourse of colonialism, the superior races have the duty to civilize the inferior. The Shikastans living on the 'Northwest fringe', a term for Europe which reverses our usual perception of the 'cradle of civilization', are 'characterized by a peculiar insensitivity to the merits of other cultures' (I,109). They thus bequeath an appalling legacy of technology and materialism to cultures 'more closely attuned with Canopus than the fringes had ever been' (I,115). Their attitude to their colonies systematizes that contempt first felt in Shikasta's early history by the rebel Giants, the 'contempt a degenerated and effete race may use for another' (I,79), the first sign of the effects of the Catastrophe on this once fine species.

The power of colonial ideology is, moreover, reinforced by religion. The materialistic religions of the fringes are 'Tools of Ruling Castes', thus persuaded that they act ' "for the good" of the conquered' (I,109–10), enslaving their bodies but saving their souls. Religious discourse constructs its own version of reality, becoming an oppressive ideology, rather than an explanatory theology when used to justify a particular economic development, such as the rise of capitalism. Like *Briefing for a Descent into Hell*, *Shikasta* shows how legends which originally came into being as ways of explaining a civilization's early history, become distorted into oppressive and rigid systems of belief. When Canopus and Sirius first jointly colonize the planet, their agents circulate 'legends and stories . . . to create mental sets' (I,34) that will prevent conflict between the different colonies. But after the Disaster, these useful teaching stories take on a new meaning for the Natives of the planet: to these primitive beings the Canopeans have such superior capacities that they can only be conceived of as gods. The Natives watch the great shining machines of the Canopean fleet lift off – in an obvious image of the Christian Ascension – confident of their imminent return. Further signs of degeneration are noted by Johor in their habit of 'bending and bowing' (I,82), apparently intoxicated by what they regard as a flattering form of worship. To attempt to halt further degeneration, Johor issues orders – commandments – which must be remembered and passed on, but these too are distorted, leaving only the idea that 'Canopus was an angry man' (I,84), whose Signature – the Bible? – must be guarded with their lives. For the first time the idea of Death becomes real, a threat and a punishment for their transgressions. Reluctant to accept responsibility – a key word in this sequence – for their own destinies, these weak creatures construct myths of salvation: they will be 'saved' from the strains of human life by 'them', the Canopean missionaries they have transformed into Gods.

In demonstrating humanity's need for myth-making, the novel itself – again like *Briefing for a Descent into Hell* – draws on myths, familiar and less familiar, to provide its own re-working of Earth history. Among the more well-known are the echoes of *Paradise Lost* in the Giants' First Disobedience of Canopean Law, which recalls both the fall of the angels and 'man's first disobedience'. The 'genetic boost' planned to halt Shikasta's further decline involves the mating of women from the 'old Davidic strain' (I,128) with what they are told are 'sacred beings', echoing both the New Testament and classical mythology. The flood which follows, the punishment of luxurious living with disruption of the wrongdoers' 'speech centres' (I,132), the destruction of the cities except for one herdsman and his tribe, all have Old Testament origins. The over-running of a vast civilization by primitive tribes which re-vitalizes an effete stock brings us into more recent history with clear reference to the Goths and Vandals, as does the 'Period of the Public Cautioners'. In this period Canopus sends down its messengers as promised, but they survive only as outcasts or in mad-houses; the religions they leave behind are distorted into mechanical dogma used by the military powers to divide and rule. While early Christianity thus appears to embody Canopean principle, its codification into the Christian Church appears to negate it.

As an alternative to these divisive ideologies, Canopus offers a plea for unity, for co-operation. During the Benevolence, the rule of the Chinese Overlords, a number of events occur which illustrate this graphically. One of George Sherban's first public acts is to be a delegate at an important Conference, where he represents three organizations: 'The Jewish Guardians of the Poor . . . The Islamic Youth Federation for the Care of the Cities . . . The United Christian Federation of Young Functionaries for Civil Care' (I,306-7). That is, George succeeds in representing interests expected to be hostile, in merging apparently irreconcilable points of view. The Conference begins with each group making routine rhetorical statements in the discourse of its own ideology, including 'routine references to running dogs of capitalism, fascist hyenas, and so-called democrats' (I,308). Having worked through the rest of the ideological repertoire, the conference ends however in unity – 'we passed without debate resolutions about unity, brotherhood, co-operation and so on.' (I,311). The presence of Canopus breaks down the verbal pigeonholes, the theoretical differences, to make room for the very real shared principles and problems. This process is enacted even more dramatically in the Mock Trial organized by the Youth Armies. In the setting of a Greek amphitheatre, designed to heighten drama, a confrontation is enacted between the White races, represented by John Brent-Oxford, and the Dark-skinned, represented by George Sherban. The trial format is a typical adversarial structure, embodying the divisive nature of ideology. Divisions are to be drawn between the innocent and guilty, defence and prosecution, those for and those against.[5] The ostensible purpose of the trial is to prove the extent of white oppression. But although Brent-Oxford pleads guilty, he also asks why the non-whites have so readily adopted the ways of the whites, blurring the distinction between the righteous and the guilty. Rumours of the possible extermination of the white races by the dark-skinned, with the approval of the Benevolence, provide further fuel for his argument.

The consequence of the Trial, therefore, – unforeseen by the Benevolence – is that the rumoured massacres never take place. The feelings that motivated them have been defused, the sense of righteousness undermined, by a new sense of agreement as to the real and urgent needs of all the nations. The whole incident is narrated by a Chinese administrator, using the eye-witness account of Tsi Kwang, a delegate quoted for the 'classic correctness of her viewpoint' (I,387). Filtered through these hostile eyes, which cannot comprehend what is taking place, it demonstrates that the control exercised by the Benevolence, the dominant power, disintegrates once it is unable to keep its subject races divided against each other.

The unity achieved at the Conference and again after the Trial is, moreover, immediately translated into action. Canopean philosophy is distinctively practical. Indeed, the novel's satirical treatment of all ideological discourse suggests it is only *by* action that individuals can

5. See also the trial that takes place in *The Sentimental Agents in the Volyen Empire*, pp. 162–86.

be judged. Johor chooses for his incarnation as a Shikastan parents who are actively involved in medical care, who regard politics as a waste of time – *doing* is what matters. When Rachel asks George for advice and direction, he tells her simply to be 'useful and efficient' (I,331). She finally appreciates the superiority of actions to words when the prospect of a new war throws her into uncertainty: she realizes that 'if George was here, what he *did* would be the answer' (I,357).

But by what criteria are actions to be judged as useful or otherwise? When Rachel suggests that 'you don't understand something until you see the results' (I,324), this smacks suspiciously of the end justifying the means, a principle which may be appropriate from a Canopean perspective, but which will hardly satisfy most modern readers. In terms of the sequence's mythic structure, what is useful is what fosters survival of those species necessary to cosmic harmony: George/Johor is interested in saving those who are 'genetically useful' (I,357). Is the sequence simply demonstrating that the human race has no choice but to forget its differences, to unite against the common enemies of war, famine and pollution? Political principles are found wanting, left and right wing alike being treated with cynicism, even contempt, making more explicit that suspicion of political commitment which began in the *Children of Violence* sequence. Is the novel suggesting that there really is no difference between Left and Right, no point in voting for one party rather than another, since all ideologies ultimately suppress truth? For many of Doris Lessing's readers this implies a disturbing rejection of political choice.

Similarly, the vision of the Canopean empire could, to some readers, be a nightmare: like the golden 'four-gated city', it could be seen as a typical artist's vision, free from human imperfection and irregularity. The cities of Rohanda before the Catastrophe are each 'a perfect artefact, with nothing in it uncontrolled'. Each individual's existence depends on 'voluntary submission to the great Whole' (I,41). He or she is only of value in so far as he or she is 'in harmony with the plan' (I,55). Families are split up and each member is sent to the most 'suitable' city, to achieve the most perfect accord between individual and environment. Canopean ideology is here inscribed in a quasi-aesthetic discourse. But because the 'Round City showed nothing that was not round', it 'could not expand' (I,47). While the inner harmonies of such a city may be perfect, the lack of room for growth suggests a static perfection at odds with the emphasis elsewhere on the principle of adaptability, and on the vitality of the margins. Canopus claims to offer to its colonies a 'newly minted, fresh, flexible method, adapted for that particular phase' (I,112), which it is the weakness of Shikastans to turn into rigid dogma. But it is not easy to feel the full force of that flexibility in the principle of 'Necessity'. The 'new freedom',[6] the unity offered as an alternative to individualism, may seem instead to be a new totalitarianism.

However, it is perhaps a mistake to assume that Canopus consistently receives authorial endorsement. The official voice of Canopus, as embodied in its histories and notes, uses an anonymous, neutral discourse which implies objectivity and detachment. It has the added authority of survival – Canopus has the wisdom to survive, unlike other planet systems which destroy themselves. It thus constitutes precisely the kind of meta-discourse, wiser than its subjects, and concealing its bias under an apparent anonymity, which has been so criticized in the guise of the omniscient narrator. And yet, like so much of Lessing's fiction, the novel to some extent undermines its own foundations. By *demonstrating* the universality of the myth-making process as it does, it opens up the possibility that what Canopus presents as history is itself myth, even that Canopus itself is a product of myth. Conversely, as the narrative moves forward in time, we imperceptibly find ourselves moving from 'myth' to what the modern reader recognizes as 'history', so that the line between the two becomes blurred. We become simultaneously conscious of the element of subjectivity in history, and of the function of myth as a metaphor for history. By the time we move into the projected future, to what we might call 'fable', questions of plausibility seem less relevant. Conflict between China and Russia has enough foundation in reality to be plausible at one level, while the change in attitude which results from the increasing supply of SOWF available to the 1 per cent of the population left after the war is consistent with the novel's mythic structure. The exact status of Canopean historiography becomes as uncertain as that of the different narratives of *The Golden Notebook*.

Moreover, while the novel begins with the voice of Canopus, it ends with a new one, the uncertain human voice of Kassim, Rachel's adopted son. But this is the human voice redeemed, enlightened by the increase of SOWF – 'here we all are *together*' (I,447, my italics). The contrast between human frailty and Canopean wisdom – so strong throughout the rest of the novel – is here reduced so that at last we have a fully human voice which commands as much respect as

6. See Lessing, 'An Ancient Way to New Freedom' in Leonard Lewin, ed., *The Elephant in the Dark* (New York: Dutton, 1976), p. 78.

Canopus. Canopus's unfailing belief that Shikasta is, after all, worth so much effort, is vindicated. The human view of a new and unfamiliar world counterbalances the previously dominant alien view of our world, to remind the reader what the novel has consistently stressed – to be ready to challenge any discourse that assumes the centre for itself.

Is the reader, then, expected to be as alert to Canopus's ideological assumptions as to those of Shikasta? Is the final irony of the novel that the reader has to deconstruct Canopus itself? Different readers will obviously answer this question in different ways. On first reading it is easy to feel that the sheer weight of 'documentary' material, extended by Johor's wisely compassionate commentary, leaves no room for dissent, to feel oppressed by Canopean righteousness. Later readings, however, bring into focus this element of questioning of the text by the text itself. If even Johor admits to subjectivity and emotionalism, can Canopus be more than the sum total of such not infallible voices?

The rest of the sequence contributes to this implicit assessment and evaluation of Canopus through the changes in focus mentioned at the beginning of this chapter. Where *Shikasta* provides a comprehensive survey of that planet's history from a distant Canopean perspective, with only occasional close-ups of particular moments of crisis when Canopean agents participate in that history, Volumes II, IV and V of the sequence maintain that close-up, from the perspective of the colonized planets or Zones themselves. Volume III is different in so far as it is narrated ostensibly from the Sirian point of view, by their agent Ambien II. Although enlightened in comparison with its subject planets, Sirius too has limitations, and the novel chronicles Ambien's conversion to the Canopean view. But the presentation of Canopus's 'inferior' colonial subjects in these later volumes throws an ambivalent and questioning light on Canopean 'perfection'.

(iii) 'The Making of the Representative for Planet 8'

The fates of Planet 8 and Shikasta are closely linked, as I explained earlier, but the narratives which recount them are very different. *The Making of the Representative for Planet 8* is a comparatively short novel, characterized by greater apparent simplicity. Dealing only with events on Planet 8 during the 'times of The Ice' (IV,11), it has a clear-cut linear narrative, while the use of a single narrator and the absence of metaphor gives the style a similar surface clarity. This absence of metaphor underlines the fact that the text as a whole should be read as a metaphor, a fable for our times.

Accordingly, like the mythical sections of *Shikasta*, the novel is free from the kind of detailed, individualistic characterization which might obscure the story-line. The narrator, although a direct participant in events, is just as undifferentiated by sex, age, family, appearance or traits of personality as the detached, wise observer of Shikasta. All we know, all we need to know, about Doeg is that he/she is a story-teller, a Memory Maker and keeper of records.[7] The emphasis is on Doeg's representative nature, as he/she describes life through 'Planet 8 eyes' (IV,26).

This is a society, moreover, in which individualism as we know it is non-existent: the individual's role in society as a whole is what matters, as it was in Rohanda's Golden Time. Planet 8 inhabitants are named according to function, rather than to confer individual identity. Only children have family names, taking adult names when they have chosen professions in harmony with their nature. For these people, one *is* what one *does* because what one *does* is determined by what one *is*. Doeg is thus not uniquely Doeg, but a representative of that function, which can be and is taken over by others.

Doeg is therefore the novel's narrator by function, rather than simply as a consequence of having a tale to tell, of bearing witness to a unique personal experience. The novel is thus more explicitly a novel about story-telling than any other in the sequence – a galactic *Golden Notebook*. Like *Shikasta*, it demonstrates the relationship between history and myth, showing how the recording of the past inevitably transforms it. When asked to recall her childhood, Alsi the Animal Keeper, becoming Doeg, comments that memory is all that remains of a life once it is over: 'It is nothing. . .a little dream' (IV,120). Living leaves such a fleeting impression that Doeg's function in recording and representing those lives is essential. But representing is *re-presenting*: Doeg is a 'Memory *Maker*': such retrospective recording is not, cannot be, the same as the past itself. Johor asks Alsi to describe herself 'as if [she] were someone else' (IV,127), emphasizing that the 'I' of the narrator is never the same as the 'I' of the narrative. She remembers on a previous occasion choosing her words so carefully that the experience has never faded from her memory:

> because she did that, made the effort to choose the right words that
> would make of her plight there along the road between farm and little

7. It is relevant to note that Doeg is also the name of the satirist poet in Dryden's *Absalom and Achitophel*.

town a sympathetic and interesting thing, so that they all . . . would come close and listen and perhaps say Poor Alsi, you must have been frightened – because of that, the incident stuck in the girl's mind, so that she can see it as clearly as if she were standing on the side of the road watching the young girl . . . (IV,129)

Similarly, travellers returning from Planet 10 describe their visit to those who stayed behind in such a way that what they tell 'becomes a story, a tale . . . legend', takes on its own life and becomes 'marvellous'. It obeys laws of its own, rather than those of the original happening.

When the coming of the ice changes their way of life beyond recognition, the past assumes even more the quality of 'tale' for those children who have no memory of life before the ice and find it hard to believe in. Since whatever is not experienced can only be understood indirectly, story-telling, metaphor, is essential to bridge the gap between the known and the unknown, past or future. Tales and legends are necessary to prepare this society under pressure for an even more stressful future.

As the history of Planet 8 is thus transformed into myth, Canopus's part in that history is also changed. Since it was Canopus who brought the inhabitants, a mongrel breed, to the Planet, Canopus is regarded as their 'maker'. When Canopus promises to save them from the ice and take them to Rohanda, their dreams of this future – so remote from present reality – take on all the qualities of unity and peace which are the traditional consolations of Heaven. Forced to use their hitherto sacrosanct ocean as a food source, they devise a ceremony of dedication which has a religious function, turning a regrettable necessity into an act of consecration. Against all reason, the people nevertheless feel at fault, since they can find no other explanation for what is happening to them. The concept of original sin is thus presented as a consequence of the species' egocentricity: all that happens in the universe must be related to itself as the centre of that universe.

The passage of time between event and retrospection thus transforms not only the event itself but the ideological perspective from which it is experienced. The coming of the ice is used by Doris Lessing, as her *Afterword* reveals, as an example of those extreme conditions which reveal and test the most fundamental assumptions of those involved. Writing about the Antarctic Expedition of Captain Scott in 1910–13, she notes, furthermore, the reassessment of the motivation and values of those early explorers that has since taken place. This process, by which the most unconscious assumptions and biases of a time are those most marvelled at later, former heresies becoming pieties and vice versa, is so important that she believes it should be studied and understood: for those happy with today's 'received opinion' and incredulous at yesterday's 'errors' may nevertheless be dogmatically dismissive of important new ideas: as Scholes puts it, 'what looks like progress to the historian is only transformation or displacement to the structuralist. Seen from its own perspective, every society has the best values, . . . but the values of one society are merely transformations of the values of another'.[8] Any dominant ideology thus marginalizes others: the ruling classes are 'identified with their own justifications for being in power' (IV,169) and therefore unable to consider the possibility that their values are not universal and eternal but relative, contingent on time and place.

And yet, since ideology is a product of circumstances, a means of explaining and justifying the conditions of one's existence, it must change with those circumstances. The rapid, extreme changes to which Planet 8 is subjected demonstrate this connection clearly. While the planet is abundant, temperate and colourful, only evolving slowly, the fruitful earth from which its inhabitants derive their existence and economic growth also symbolizes their ideals – 'solidity, immobility, permanence'. The inhabitants are likewise 'bound in continuity': 'this was only how we with our Planet 8 eyes had to see things' (IV,26). Once the material conditions of their existence enter into a state of rapid change, however, their perception changes accordingly, so that they soon recognize there is no such thing as permanence. Instead they cherish and identify with the ocean, a symbol of wholeness derived from 'rapid and easy interchange'. Experience determines what one is able to see and understand, and Planet 8 eyes learn to see differently, as their bodies too learn to survive on a carnivorous diet and to support heavy garments to keep out the cold. This process of adaptation to each change in the environment leads ultimately to the bodily death of the Representatives – the last survivors: gazing at each other 'for the last time with [their] old eyes', they move into a condition where they see 'with eyes [they] had not known [they] possessed'. Instead of a 'steady perspective' (IV,156–7), this new vision resists the fixity and stasis of ideology, perceiving movement and space, where before had been immobility and solidity.

This ability to adopt shifting perspectives is symbolized by the

8. Scholes, *Structuralism*, p. 195.

microscope, which introduces change into a basically static society even before the coming of the ice. It brings about changes in education, which becomes a centralized and professional process in order for all the children to have access to the instrument. This new eye introduces the knowledge that there is no such thing as solidity, only dancing atoms surrounded by space – 'A dance that you modify by how you observe it' (IV,91). Reality, it is once again asserted, is not a fixed condition, but changes according to the situation of the perceiver. This state of constant flux requires of those who inhabit it adaptability and openness, not ideological blinkers.

The microscope also reveals, as the epigram for *Briefing for a Descent into Hell* suggests, unforeseen relationships which make possible a new understanding of what constitutes a whole. The dance of atoms that is a single human being can be broken down into individual elements which are each capable of being considered a 'whole' (IV,87). This scientific image thus reinforces the sequence's philosophical stance, providing a fresh basis for Lessing's recurrent emphasis on the delusory dangers of individualism. When Doeg laments the difficulty of conveying intensely personal feelings and dreams in words, and the resultant sense of loneliness, Johor retorts, 'do you imagine that you spin dreams out of yourself that are uniquely yours' in that 'shared sleep?' (IV,83–4). Such arrogance has to give way to an understanding that consciousness, like unconsciousness, is shared. Even when Doeg calls 'the feeling of *me*', a unique chance of genetic accident, is shared (IV,111). Doeg is therefore constantly meeting his 'self', since that self is not his physical incarnation, but 'part of a whole much larger than oneself' (IV,114). Doeg envisages the possibility that, from Johor's point of view, the whole species consists of parts who 'share a quality that makes them . . . one', just as each part of the individual body bears the same genetic coding. Once Doeg acquires this understanding, he earns the right to escape the grim reality of Planet 8 and return to 'the light from which we all come' (IV,82). Humanity's only salvation, it appears, lies in erasing personal subjectivity, in relinquishing the idea of a unified, autonomous individual self.

For this kind of 'splitting' of the self is also a transcendence of the self, such as fascinates Doris Lessing in the early explorers. When the little white rodents which were brought back from the Pole die, Johor insists that 'their qualities will be reborn' (IV,109), even if that particular species dies out. As Doeg learns what it means to be a 'Representative', and that his essential quality as Doeg is his function, then he recognizes that he cannot disappear, just as 'Alsi cannot disappear since Alsi is and must be continually re-created' (IV,145). Theoretical understanding becomes experience when, on dying physically, the Representatives see 'the vast space that had been what in fact [they] mostly were . . . a unity . . . patterns of matter . . . feelings, and thought, and will' (IV,157–8). Their physical substance, which is just one of those patterns, decomposes into the substance of Planet 8, while a different pattern goes on. This is the 'Making of the Representative for Planet 8', a being that is 'one, but a conglomerate of individuals' (IV,159). Dissolved into these elements, the split self can truly live in the life of the whole.

But while Canopus – in the person of Johor – is thus shown to be a trustworthy guide through this bewildering process of change, the deification of Canopus discussed earlier is presented as a weakness. For the belief in a pact with Canopus leads to inevitable horror and loss of purpose when the promise of salvation is apparently not fulfilled. Instead of the expected airlift, Canopus delivers food and shelter. As the climatic situation worsens and the inhabitants of Planet 8 lose control and understanding of their environment, dependence on 'our Saviour and Maker Canopus' (IV,62) grows. They abrogate all responsibility for self-help, neglecting the present as they seek escape in their dreams of heaven. When the Wall which Canopus instructed them to build as protection from the ice collapses, their desolation is essentially of their own making. Their sense that the impossible has happened, because 'Canopus had been wrong' (IV,131), is a consequence of their turning Canopus into an infallible deity. It is not so much Canopus that has proved to be wrong, but their perception of Canopus. Its promises of safety were contingent on circumstances that were beyond its control. Canopus is not God, not an omnipotent creator, but itself part of another system – a 'creation and creatures' (IV,79). The inhabitants of Planet 8 are not therefore 'victims of [its] perfection' (IV,80), as Doeg suggests in a moment of bitterness, but victims of their own mythology. The novel thus implies that the authority of Canopus is in part a construction of its colonies, of the margins themselves, raising more questions about its status and the extent to which it receives authorial validation.

(iv) 'Documents Relating to the Sentimental Agents in the Volyen Empire'

The final volume in the sequence shifts the focus to the furthest margins of the galaxy of Argos, to the Volyen Empire, independent of

Canopus. The Volyen Empire is plagued by instability. Vast population increases caused by a cosmic disturbance – due in turn to conflict in the Sirian Empire – result in a series of invasions, each planet in turn overthrowing and invading others, enslaving its inhabitants and establishing short-lived and repressive regimes. When Sirius itself invades as a punishment, it leaves the 'agents' referred to in the novel's title, converts to the Sirian cause. They are 'sentimental' because victims of emotionalism: while paying lip-service to Sirius, they have in fact so lost touch with the home planet that the reality of Sirius means nothing to them (V,154). In spite of this important Sirian presence, however, once again it is Canopus's perspective that dominates the novel, as most of the events taking place are narrated by a Canopean agent, Klorathy, writing to Johor on Canopus. But what is striking about this volume is its humour, in particular its satirical presentation of the theme that binds the whole sequence – the ideological function of language.

For this novel finally makes explicit what is implicit in the earlier volumes: that language is the key to those important mechanisms by which one set of assumptions and values dominates or gives way to another, those mechanisms that we need to understand 'so that we are not controlled by them' (V,170). It explores the nature of rhetoric, words devoid of real meaning, but with the power to trigger off intense reflex emotional responses. As Rhetoric is such a useful tool for 'the father of lies', Canopus's enemy Shammat has a 'School of Rhetoric' on Volyen. This takes two forms, one a theological seminary, the other a school of politics, but both teach equally misleading types of discourse. Such discourse conceals, for instance, the true motives of colonialism – even from the colonizers: Ormarin, leader of a rebellious faction in the Volyen Empire, is able to distract attention, including his own, from the conquering minority's exploitation of the slave population by representing the 'underdog' sections of the conquering minority and articulating their grievances. He acts as an image of the kind of white trade unionist, fighting to protect his members from the competition offered by black workers, who featured in Lessing's earliest fiction. In Shammat's school 'verbal formulations' (V,68) can be learned, to produce intensely felt but unreasoning responses and behaviour. For Rhetoric works on the emotions, making it a useful tool for all those who wish to manipulate others. Most of the students who pass through Shammat's school fail because of their own excessive emotional response: Krogul – Shammat's representative on Volyen – advises them that they 'must learn to use words but not be used by them'

(V,86). He himself, with his 'dedicated persona', is a skilled orator, easily manipulating others with words alone.

The inhabitants of the Volyen Empire seem to know nothing but rhetoric. Even Sirius is not immune. Unlike Canopus, which early in its history discovered the Necessity that enables them to develop a thriving, balanced Empire, Sirius instead 'developed Rhetoric': 'Each new planet, each attractive new morsel of property, was swallowed to the accompaniment of words, words, words, describing theft as a gift, destruction as development, murder as public hygiene. The patterns of words, ideas, changed as Sirius grew a conscience and agonized through its long ages of change . . . always, always justifying what they did with new patterns of words.' (V,95)

Rhetoric is thus not simply, as Krogul suggests, a means of manipulating others, but a process by which subjects are enabled to conceal from themselves their own real motives. As such it is an essential tool of ideology. For language, as we have seen, is the means by which the subject is constructed. Illustrating the argument by further reference to the ill-fated Shikasta, Klorathy recalls the ideological tyranny exerted by religion for 2,000 years, only to be replaced by politics: because Shikastans 'had been conditioned by the various sects of that religion to need domination, "priests", creeds, dogmas, ukases, they sought these things again, in the same forms but under other names, notably in "politics" ' (V,101). The conclusion is inevitable: 'freedom is not possible to people who have been conditioned to need tyrannies' (V,128). Those like Incent who succumb to an 'attack of Rhetoric' (V,11), lose their capacity for independent rational thought. As subjects of rhetorical discourse, they become subjected to the ideology inscribed in that rhetoric. Instead of using words, they are used by them. While young Volyens may see through this deceit, with the need to earn a living comes the need to be accepted as a member of the governing class and thus to conform (V,102). Further conformity to more specific 'verbal formulations' is demanded as the price of acceptance in further sub-groups, outside of which these individuals are unable to function. Even those who reject the rhetoric of Empire 'become prisoners of the Rhetoric of oppositional groups whose only aim is to become, in their turn, rulers who will govern through Rhetoric. Through the formulations and manipulations of words' (V,102). In the analysis of Sirius which follows this quotation, Lessing clearly refers to the Soviet Union – an image of Utopia for thousands of young idealists who treat all news of its brutal realities as unfortunate deviation from the 'correct path' (V,105), while that tyranny suppresses all internal critics through imprisonment or torture. The disillusionment with left-wing politics noticed in my discussion of *Shikasta* speaks more clearly here than ever.

To combat the effects of rhetoric, victims like the Canopean agent Incent who succumb to its effects have to be transferred to the Hospital for Rhetorical Diseases on Volyendesta, one of the Volyen moons. The hospital is otherwise known as 'the Institute for Historical Studies', for only immersion in the lived historical experience can make the patient aware of the realities concealed by the ideological counters of Rhetoric. The Hospital uses numerous historical examples of rhetoric as a means of *de-sensitizing* and re-educating its victims. By this means the novel satirizes the rhetorics used to sustain the different political and religious systems which were themselves satirized in *Shikasta*. Its targets include the nationalistic rhetorics that motivate the opposing armies of World War I and II, the rhetoric of the 'Polshan' (Polish) cause which sustains its 'dramatic and even self-immolating nature' (V,20), the 'elevated language of the Constitution of the Volyen "Empire", which promises happiness, freedom, and justice to every one of its citizens as inherent, inalienable rights' (V,22–23) – an obvious reference to the American Constitution – and the Churchillian rhetoric of 'We shall fight them on the beaches' (V,28). What all have in common is the use of words misleading enough to drive millions to self-destruction against all reason or the instincts of self-preservation.

However, these attempts by Canopus to harden its agents against the effects of rhetoric lead Klorathy to wonder whether Canopus does not overestimate the power of reason, since the language of reason is so weak in comparison with the language of rhetoric (V,56): when Krogul speaks to a crowd of workers, incensing them against Grice, Volyen's minion, Klorathy himself feels affected: 'Oh, how small and meagre and pitiful suddenly seemed to me all our efforts, above all our language, so cool and measured and *chosen*' (V,60). Klorathy further suggests that, because of their use of such language, Canopean agents lack persuasive power over the inhabitants of other planets, to whom they appear 'indifferent and passionless' (V,60). And yet the reader may remember that, when the inhabitants of Planet 8 ask Johor whether he really means what he says, he replies, 'Does Canopus . . . deal in rhetoric?' (IV,78), posing a question that is itself so ironically rhetorical that it undermines its own surface meaning. It appears that even Canopus is not immune from the blinkers of ideology. Even Canopean understanding may be limited by its own assumptions and values.

The novel ends enigmatically – in mid-sentence – raising a number of questions not only about itself, but about the sequence as a whole. Incent has had another relapse, a warning of the need for constant vigilance over the words we use and hear. Even Canopean agents can become the 'sentimental agents' of the novel's title. Ormarin, of whom so much is hoped, suffers from an attack of 'What Is the Point-ism, or The Futility of All Effort' (V,68), losing sight of Canopean practicality. His 'overindulgence in irony' (V,69) paralyses him. The vulnerability of these agents is, moreover, dealt with in a humorous satirical style which reflects back on the earlier presentation of Canopus, counteracting the prophetic, solemn tones of the first volume. Given Doris Lessing's readiness to use the endings of her fiction to force us into a radical revision of our previous reading, this ending is surely a warning not to take Canopus too seriously, or to assume that it represents the author's point of view.

The final volume therefore seems to me to offer a witty but pertinent footnote to guide the act of reading, assuming that the sequence is read as a whole. But the complex structural and verbal ironies involved in such an interpretation will not be equally apparent to every reader. I am encouraged in this view of the sequence by its title: *Canopus in Argos* reminds us that Canopus is only part of a greater system, a system which takes its name from the galley which searched for the Golden Fleece of mythology – an image of quest, not of static perfection. Like Martha Quest's ideal golden city, and the Golden Notebook, such images of quest should not be confused with the idea that the grail has been found. But does the sequence as a whole open up sufficiently the possibility of Canopean fallibility? If there is, as I have suggested, a sense of contradiction, of tension, between the dominant role of Canopean values in the sequence, and the sequence's fairly systematic undermining of its own myths, is this tension finally resolved in a form of mystical escapism offered by the very potent image of Canopus, as many reviews of the sequence would suggest?

To answer this question we need, I think, to consider the metaphorical quality of these texts, which I have suggested resides in the text as a whole, rather than in the language employed. Lessing explains that she 'went off into metaphor' because of the difficulty of finding words in the English language for 'mystical' areas of experience, other than those already appropriated by particular schools of psychology or philosophy.[9] Words like 'collective unconscious' are not as 'open', exploratory or tentative in meaning as she requires. More indirect forms of

9. Television interview, BBC 2, 7 May 1980.

expression may avoid the tram-lining of language into unitary, univocal meaning characteristic of realist, rational discourse. However, the forms of these novels – with the exception of *Shikasta* – creates other problems in relation to meaning. While *The Making of the Representative for Planet 8*, for instance, overtly suggests that change is essential, indeed inevitable, since 'nothing can be static' (IV,152), its metaphorical form seems to undermine that 'message'.

For metaphor is a figure of speech based on *similarity*: one thing represents another on the basis of a perceived likeness. Metaphoric tales can be said to have universal, eternal significance: the world of Planet 8 or Volyen can be said to stand for any other at a time of crisis, their few individual elements condensed into general, abstract qualities. There results, therefore, a tension between the urgency of the text's themes and the sense of timelessness generated by its form.

This tension is, I think, linked to the hostility to politics already noticed in this sequence. Toril Moi sums up the problem in her analysis of feminist Utopian writing: 'signalling the repressive effects of the social structures that give rise to the utopia in the first place, its gaps and inconsistencies indicate the pervasive nature of the authoritarian ideology the utopian thinker is trying to undermine'.[10] I have already indicated some of the inconsistencies in Lessing's Canopean myth, and its potentially authoritarian aspects. Cut off from temporality – with the exception of Shikasta – the worlds of the Argos galaxy are disengaged from the political issues involved in any analysis of contemporary civilization. The sequence can be seen as a totally radical rejection of existing structures and ideologies, made possible by the mythic, sci-fi form. But it can also be seen as an evasive, even reactionary, fantasy, since the only answer to the tensions it engenders appears to be a flight from social reality. For many readers this sequence represents a disappointing withdrawal from the realities so forcefully conveyed in the author's analysis of repressive ideological structures.

Challenging as the 'Archives' are, therefore, in presenting a more radical critique of Western civilization than may be possible within the realist tradition, they present an ambiguous view of authoritarian systems and give less voice to those marginalized by such systems. This effect is, I think, linked to the absence of that 'female' perspective characteristic of Doris Lessing's earlier fiction. This is not to imply an essentialist view of gender – that all women share such a perspective by virtue of their shared biological functions – but simply to reiterate

10. Moi is here paraphrasing Arnhelm Neususs. See *Textual Politics*, p. 122.

what I have already argued. Many of the 'alternative' values embodied in the earlier work are those traditionally labelled 'female' and accordingly marginalized by a patriarchal culture. The Canopus sequence upholds those values in so far as it rejects the categorical, divisive discourse of political and religious ideologies, and its very form implicitly challenges the rationalist, humanist values inscribed in the forms of realist fiction. But the alternative order it offers has a potentially authoritarian dimension which seems to turn away from the openness and multiplicity of meaning and value which many see as the strengths of Lessing's work.

6

Return to Earth: *The Good Terrorist*

It may not be surprising that, after experiments in 'inner-space fiction', science fiction and fantasy of various kinds, Doris Lessing should return to the subject of contemporary Britain. It is more surprising, perhaps, that the novel which marks this return – *The Good Terrorist* – should have so much in common with her first novel, *The Grass is Singing*. In being both 'good' and a 'terrorist', the novel's heroine, Alice Mellings, dramatically exemplifies that splitting of the subject which was first shown in Mary Turner. Both novels demonstrate the inseparability of the personal and the political, but whereas *The Grass is Singing* considers this relationship in terms of sexual identity and racial identity, *The Good Terrorist* is concerned with sexual ideology and class consciousness, or more specifically Marxist ideology as interpreted by the radical splinter group to which Alice belongs. It demonstrates, that is, the ideological processes which construct the 'good terrorist'.

(i) Sexual Identity: The Good Daughter

Although a thirty-six-year-old woman at the time of the novel's action, Alice is shown to be haunted by a sense of loss and insecurity – a feeling that 'had been with her since she could remember: being excluded, left out. Unwanted' (p. 101). This can be identified in Lacanian terms as the consequence of the infant's loss of that sense of undifferentiated unity characteristic of the 'imaginary', pre-Oedipal phase, and of the sense of separation from the mother. Its origin is made clear when Alice recalls, amongst her strongest memories, being sent to sleep elsewhere when her parents held parties, so that she felt she had no place in her own home. The sense of separation from her mother is evident in her jealousy of her mother's friendships, which seem to 'exclude everyone else' (p. 322). This insecurity generates Alice's most compelling desires, personal and political.

But this sense of exclusion is most intensified by her awareness of her parents' sexual intimacy. When during other parties, she is forced to sleep in their room, she is conscious of feeling both excluded and 'violently emotional' (p. 214) because this confrontation with their sexuality arouses feelings she cannot admit to – those taboo desires for the parent which are repressed into the unconscious. Like Mary Turner before her marriage, Alice represses her sexuality by refusing in a sense to grow up, to become a woman: she has the 'pudgy, formless' look that characterizes both the pubertal girl and the middle-aged woman, 'heavy and cautious, and anxious to please' (pp. 11–12). Even when visiting the revolutionaries in the next-door squat, the well-brought-up 'girl', as she is so often called, wears her 'nice blouse with the small pink flowers and the neat round collar' (p. 162). The anger she remembers feeling towards her mother for telling her about menstruation in her 'earth-motherish way' (p. 233), is only explicable as a response to having forced onto her attention a sexual reality that she wishes to ignore. She justifies this as a feminist refusal to let 'anything so tedious' get in her way. Yet this is clearly a rationalization, as is evident from the feelings of threat, disgust and exclusion she experiences whenever made conscious of the sexual relationships of the other members of the commune. Similarly, when Andrew Connors, the Russian agent at No. 45, shows sexual interest in her, he arouses 'waves of sensation', of both fascination and disgust (p. 228).

Alice deals with Connors' approaches by retreating into the two female roles that she does find acceptable – first she becomes 'like a child', weeping, and finally rejects him 'in a tidy, housewifely way' (pp. 229–30). For the force of her forbidden desires has been displaced onto socially approved goals. Alice's conforming self tries both to gain the approval of the mother whose rejection she so fears, and to conform to a cultural ideal which will confer acceptance and value. Accordingly, she usually approaches Dorothy Mellings with the 'timid, anxious-to-please smile of the good daughter' (p. 321), whatever hostility she feels towards her mother in her absence. This role combines the traditional female qualities validated by the patriarchal order – the domestic virtues of the housewife and the submissiveness of the child – while eliminating the potentially threatening sexual element.

Alice's desire for union with her mother is thus displaced onto identification with her mother, as she enacts the role of 'good-girl Alice, her mother's daughter' (p. 131). Although Dorothy wanted an education and a career for her daughter, Alice instead simply repeats her mother's life of 'cooking and nannying' (p. 329), just as Mary Turner repeats her mother's. The fantasy self to which Alice aspires is not only the ideal daughter, but the ideal mother which was denied her. Her identification with her mother thus only functions in relation to Dorothy *as* mother, to the warm nurturing Dorothy, not to her mother as a person. For Dorothy is also the person by whom Alice feels rejected, an object of hostility and 'rage', giving Alice 'red-hot hands', and inducing her to 'explode' (p. 130). Resenting her mother's desire for privacy and her sexuality, both of which she experiences as exclusion, Alice determines to be different: feeling guilty about wanting to be alone, she suppresses any individual needs which interfere with the fulfilment of the maternal ideal, like the most conventional of women. The role of the good mother, like that of the good daughter, thus reinforces the repression of her sexuality.

For Alice's adult life has been spent helping others, sheltering them, feeding them, in the best tradition of the self-sacrificing mother: we are told she was her happiest as a 'housemother' in a Manchester commune. Happiness is sitting at the head of the kitchen table, pouring coffee for her 'family'. Alice is like a mother to Jim, the unemployed black youth who was the original inhabitant of the squat, and to Philip, the craftsman whose skill is no protection against exploitation by employers and bureaucrats. All Alice's emotional energies go into nonsexual relationships, the most important being her love for Jasper, whose homosexuality erases any sexual threat. He has the thin, graceful body of 'a small boy', arousing her maternal, protective feelings. And yet she refuses to acknowledge the inequality of the relationship, comparing it to a marriage on the rare occasions that Jasper talks things over with her in their separate sleeping-bags before they fall asleep. Theirs is a parody of a heterosexual relationship, in which Alice is pitifully grateful for the smallest gesture of affection, feeling a 'surge of delight, of gratitude' when he suggests, 'Saturday night we could go and paint up a few slogans' (p. 100), the revolutionary's equivalent of painting the town red.

But as indicated in earlier chapters, identification *with* can only proceed by way of identification *against*. In identifying with the mother, the good daughter suppresses all that is culturally identified as 'male' – authority, dominance, aggression. This process is reinforced in Alice's case by her father's separation from her mother and acquisition of a new family. Because Alice's feelings of aggression are repressed, she can only explode inwardly: her anger lives inside. Only in isolated, private moments do these repressed emotions emerge in 'banging . . . grunting, whining, snarling noises' (p. 123). Aligned with the female, marginalized by the patriarchal order, Alice thus identifies with the powerless. 'The look' of suffering which so enrages Jasper, the homosexual youth she loves and lives with, is the outward expression of a sense of helplessness which can lead only to passive despair or the rage of frustration.

Because they are repressed, Alice's most intense desires are only evident in metaphoric substitutions. The sense of unity and security last experienced through the mother is projected onto houses – an obvious symbol of the womb. The first such substitution is logically her mother's own house, the home of Alice's childhood, so that Alice feels 'furious, betrayed, deadly' (p. 184) when her mother sells it, removing all possibility of Alice's return to childhood safety. Once sold, 'just abandoned' by her mother, it becomes herself, 'abandoned long ago' (p. 204). Now she has 'no real home' (p. 213). She therefore transfers the feelings invested in it to the squat which she attempts to transform into a home of her own. Her heart is 'full of pain' when she first sees this 'beautiful and unloved house' (p. 5), since its neglected and condemned state arouses a 'passionate identification' with it (p. 25). Filling the kitchen with the bowls of fruit and flowers that are for her 'the symbol of happiness', she makes it once more the centre of a family – '*her family*' (pp. 78–9) of unemployed, homeless misfits and self-styled revolutionaries. When this house too has to be abandoned, the 'poor house' is in Alice's eyes '*betrayed*' (p. 365), as she has been. The house is a particularly effective symbol in the novel, since the reader is made aware not only of its specific significance for Alice, but of its full potential as a signifier. For although it is the site of both the 'great table' and the 'large bed', Alice acknowledges only the potency of the former as a symbol of unity, a focus for the domestic and maternal aspirations of the good daughter. The reader is therefore again alerted to all that she represses, all that is part of 'her buried self . . . her secret breathing body which she ignored for nearly all of her time' (p. 198).

(ii) Class Consciousness: The Terrorist

In addition to her sexual identity, however, Alice has a political identity which is generated by the discourse of class conflict. For Alice is not the subject of a single discourse, a single ideology, but the site where different kinds of discourse meet. As sexual and political ideology create different, often conflicting desires in her, this further contributes to the splitting of her psyche, her political identity bringing into play the self repressed by the good daughter.

Just as Mary Turner, through the discourse of white racism, is identified with the 'master race', although a woman, so Alice's education as a middle-class daughter gives her access to the discourse of reason, argument and authority, and therefore entry into the male symbolic order. She speaks the same language as the authorities who determine the fates of the less powerful, the less educated. Her voice is as 'peremptory, as dismissive' as the voice of the bureaucrats who will decide what happens to 'her' house (p. 87). Jim is 'incredulous' at the ease with which she deals with the police in her 'clear reasonable tones' (p. 70), since this is not a skill that unemployed working-class blacks like himself have at their disposal. She is essentially a 'middle-class girl with her assurance, her knowledge of the ropes' (p. 23). For Alice has also inevitably imbibed many of the values and assumptions inscribed in the discourse of the educated bourgeoisie. At the more trivial and humorous level is her 'prim' concern with dietary habits – she cannot eat chips without worrying about cholesterol – and even in a house without hot water, she washes her face and brushes her hair. Similarly, both Jasper and Andrew Connors accuse her, on the evidence of her transformation of the squat, of a 'bourgeois' concern for comfort and cleanliness. More seriously symptomatic is her attitude towards Monica, a homeless mother, to whom she says, 'You have to do something for yourself, you know' (p. 136). This stand-on-your-own-two-feet stance indicates the gulf in the experience and attitudes of the two women. Jim and Monica are working-class victims, whose pitifully low expectations limit both their aspirations and their ability to achieve them; in contrast, Alice and her friends are, according to Alice's mother, spoiled children: they have always assumed that they should get what they want. Alice's instinctive suspicion that, if she found Monica somewhere to live, 'she'd muck it all up somehow' (p. 138) indicates an identity with the dominant order which she would prefer to repudiate.

For Alice rejects this middle-class identity with the same violent intensity with which she represses her sexuality, finding the consumerism of that class disgusting, and refusing to live a 'bourgeois' life even as a cover for the subversive work Connors wishes her to undertake. She pursues an imaginary 'revolutionary' self that derives its identity from solidarity with the working-class. Preferring to ignore the revulsion with which individual representatives of the working class so often inspire her, Alice is fixated on the idea of the 'people', a notional entity which will come into being when the capitalist system is overthrown. She prides herself on being only 'one generation away from working-class' (p. 255) on her mother's side, and is proud of her father's beginnings as a self-educated man from the North, politically committed to the Left. Yet she now despises his financial success, classifying him with other 'bloody liberals and revisionists . . . bourgeois trash' (p. 202). She is, however, unable to apply this distinction between working-class origins and working-class life-style and attitudes to herself. She seems unable to see that although, as her mother's daughter, she may have working-class origins, when her mother speaks, 'so authoritatively and naturally from Alice's mouth', it is in her middle-class 'good hostess manner' (p. 301), even when entertaining a man she believes to be a Russian agent. Class is not simply a matter of birth or conscious choice, but of discourse. She is ironically relieved to find that this same man, Peter Cecil, is in fact from MI5, '*One of us*' (p. 367), as she puts it. While attributing this sense of a shared identity to his Englishness, Alice is unconsciously acknowledging the claims of that middle-class self outraged by the rebellious political self and its working-class identity.

The contradictions Alice experiences in pursuing a class identity are shared by the other revolutionaries in the squat. Despising the middle classes who enjoy their domestic comforts without knowing what efforts these comforts cost, they assert that all such comfort 'comes from the workers, from *us*' (p. 57), and adopt fake working-class accents to lend authenticity to their pose. Yet this identification is clearly theoretical rather than real, since they show little understanding of the working-class members of the squat or of those, like Monica, who wish to join them. The concept of work itself has no appeal, whether it is paid employment or the work involved in the restoration and upkeep of the house. Their attitude towards the workers is like that of the benevolent white colonialist, inherently paternalistic: they know better than the workers themselves what the workers need: the 'ordinary people' do not understand what the revolutionaries are trying to do on 'their' behalf. The gulf between them and those they claim to speak for is implicitly recognized by the workers themselves, who are hostile to the idea of 'students and layabouts' joining their picket.

However, unlike the 'split' Alice, the rest of the comrades are predominantly the subjects of a single discourse, a rigid theoretical discourse which gives them a superior attitude towards those who cannot or do not wish to use it: even Alice is told that ideology is not her 'line', because she tends to use phrases like 'human nature' which are simply 'beyond the pale' (p. 95). Characters like Jasper and Bert find it difficult to communicate without using the discourse of the political meeting, in which the presence and point of view of others is 'reported' and either 'acknowledged' or 'dismissed' (pp. 8–9), according to whether it conforms to the group's current policy 'formulations'. In this way divergent points of view can be rejected without having to be measured against any kind of reality. For the discourse of the comrades is characterized by its remoteness from reality. Unlike Connors, 'the real thing' (p. 115), who acts with cool detachment, these 'amateurs' are driven by intense emotions, but attempt to evade this fact by using theoretical language which conceals the real cause of their identification with the working classes.

For this identification has its roots, like Alice's, in childhood. Alice herself is contemptuous of the tendency she has observed for all communes to sit around discussing their 'shitty childhoods' (p. 121). Her comrades are repeatedly compared to children by characters as different as Dorothy Mellings and Andrew Connors. The comparison is validated by the discomfort they all experience when meeting in the former nursery at No. 45, where they are disturbed by 'the ghosts of privileged children – of loved children' (p. 176), implicitly aware of their own emotional deprivation. The life histories of individual comrades further support this image. Alice blames Jasper's mother for his 'lost child' manner, while he himself focuses his venom on his father. Faye, the lesbian, demonstrates the splitting of the subject in tragic form: adopting the manner of a little girl because it is 'hard for her to assert herself' (p. 105), her 'other self' is an 'awful, violent Faye . . . prisoner of the pretty cockney' (p. 30), who speaks with the voice of deprivation and suffering. A battered baby, 'just like a child' herself (p. 120), she is hysterical when faced with the request to house the homeless mother and child, too painfully reminded of her own past, and thereby alerting the reader to the true motives behind her rage.

For if anger has its source in childhood, the rage felt by the child at the frustration of its desires cannot safely be unleashed on the parents, upon whom the child is dependent. It must therefore be displaced or repressed. Alice's 'clear hot anger' (p. 17) can be justified on behalf of others, rather than being exposed as a personal indulgence inducing a sense of shame. She can evade the real roots of her anger, the recognition that 'the people' neglected by the state who arouse her pity are a metaphoric substitute for herself, the unloved child. Throughout the novel, it is refusal or rejection by her parents which triggers off much of Alice's rage. When her father, for instance, refuses to act as guarantor for the squat's electricity bill, she is filled with 'hot red waves of murder' (p. 142). She feels a similar desire to blow up her mother's new flat, unable to bear either her mother's reduced circumstances – for which she is partly responsible – or the loss of her old home.

For these revolutionaries, then, the political serves personal ends, as Alice implicitly acknowledges when she decides to hold a Communist Central Union Congress to improve the atmosphere in the house. This repression of their true motives not only renders their aims suspect, but makes them incapable of the kind of analysis which would make coherent, meaningful political activity possible. The 'Union', as Connors points out, is totally lacking in 'responsibility', individual or collective – that quality so valued by Canopus. Nowhere is this more evident than in the bombing which is their most important public act, the expression of their 'murderous' need to 'prove their power' (p. 314). Faye's 'it serves them right' (p. 346) epitomizes their reaction to the possible loss of life, turning this 'political statement' into an attention-seeking act of childish revenge.

In Alice's case, these personal ends are made very clear. Her political identity as a member of the CCU, based on the 'great traditions of the British working class' (p. 219), liberates her repressed, angry 'male' self. Just as Mary Turner found that, when taking on Dick's role as master, she was able to turn her repressed anger against the natives, so Alice's role as 'revolutionary' enables the anger repressed by the 'good daughter' to be turned against authority. 'The look' that embodies her sense of helplessness is thus banished, since anger produces in her 'waves of energy' which make her 'alive and tingling' (p. 145). When spray painting with Jasper she writes her anger onto the walls, inscribing onto the public domain that angry self she cannot give full vent to in her private life. Alice's political purpose not only displaces and releases this rage, but confers approval on the repressed self, legitimizing the full force of her anger.

The battle against authority similarly provides a release through substitution for Alice's repressed sexuality. There is a suggestion of sexual heat in the burning imagery attaching to her anger and in her face which at such times 'swelled and shone' (p. 22). The link is made more explicit during her confrontations with the police, powerful representatives of authority, and more specifically with male police: when she senses the restrained brutality of the police who visit the squat, she feels 'sharp little thrills down her thighs' (p. 69). At demonstrations she longs for the 'rough violence' of the policeman's hands, anticipating how she will 'let herself go limp' (p. 237). Her relationship with Jasper, when it is not depicted in maternal terms, bears similar masochistic overtones, since any sign of her distress meets with angry commands and his painful circling of her wrist with his 'hard bone' (p. 5), in turn inflaming her anger and hence her recovery.

However, there is a price to be paid for this 'liberation' of Alice's repressed self. To retain the approval of her comrades, she has to conform to their ideology, which, as I have already suggested, is in many ways an ironic reflection of the dominant symbolic order. This is particularly evident in the prevailing attitude towards the female, which is linked with their attitude towards manual labour, both of which they implicitly devalue. The women in the commune carry out most of the manual labour connected with the house, as well as the traditional caring functions, and provide emotional support for each other. In this context, 'two women at work on a roof' (p. 86) are not an image of liberation from sexual stereotyping, as one might assume, so much as an indication of the way that women and manual labour are similarly marginalized, while the men are usually to be found waiting, 'talking politics' (p. 39). Like Mary Turner, Alice shows complicity in patriarchal ideology by subscribing to those discursive practices which devalue the caring, practical activities traditionally carried out by women, thus devaluing her own skills and strengths. She abuses Bob Hood, the council official, by comparing him to 'a fucking housewife' (p. 89), and when herself left alone, cleaning the house, she regards those out picketing as engaged in more 'serious' work. Envious of them, imagining them shouting 'the workers united' (p. 80), she has apparently no more consciousness of irony than they themselves possess. She is even 'apologetic', 'guilty' about staying behind, as much a victim of patriarchal ideology as any housewife confronted with the question 'What have you been doing all day?' In the world of the revolutionary, therefore, Alice ironically assumes a role that is traditionally 'female' in its passive acceptance of male authority. Her 'private stream' of thoughts is continually silenced because Jasper 'would not have authorized it' (p. 8). Her thoughts and feelings are censored in 'submission to higher powers' (p. 134), her predominantly male comrades.

Because Alice is split into two such irreconcilable selves, she is capable of experiencing both 'violent derision' and 'another current, of want, of longing' when faced with a street full of suburban houses (p. 24). Likewise, in her relationship with her mother, desire for her mother's approval brings the 'good daughter' into operation, while her sense of rejection by her mother arouses the rage of the rebellious self. Her psyche has therefore to devise strategies to keep her two selves separate, so that she can scream abuse at her mother for her bourgeois vices, and in the next moment ask for her help, with no feeling of awkwardness. Her most effective strategy is simply to forget inconvenient facts: she forgets having been told that her mother is selling her home, forgets having informed the Samaritans that a bomb has been planted by the IRA. These acts of denial are attempts by one self to repudiate the other.

Such processes can lead only to unreality and fantasy of the kind that precedes mental instability and breakdown. While *The Good Terrorist* does not take the reader so far into this process as *The Grass is Singing* does, it indicates the inevitable consequence. The bombing with which it ends is the most extreme manifestation of Alice's revolutionary self, terrifying the conforming self, and imposing impossible strains on this faculty for denial. Yet feeling 'severed from her mother' who will be 'finally repudiating her' because of the bombing, she tells herself that 'she hadn't *really* been part of it' (pp. 366, 368). Alice attempts to deal with the situation by constructing a fantasy in which her rational, 'good daughter' self feels 'in command of everything again' (p. 370): she imagines herself becoming friends with Peter Cecil, the man from MI5, united by their shared Englishness, while also persuading herself that she can prevent Gordon O'Leary, the terrorist, from finding his 'material' by hiding it in the attic.[1] Where the revolutionary self had been pushing the 'good daughter' into the background, the conforming self – fighting for survival – now attempts to bury the revolutionary self, to deny its existence.

As always when faced with problems she cannot cope with, Alice retreats into her safe place inside, discovered in childhood, into the story of the 'good girl' Alice (p. 368). At the end of the novel she therefore looks like 'a nine-year-old girl who has had, perhaps, a bad

---

1. Lessing here uses the image central to the analysis of women's writing carried out by Sandra Gilbert and Susan Gubar in *'The Madwoman in the Attic': The Woman Writer and the Nineteenth-Century Imagination* (Yale University Press, 1979). Gilbert and Gubar suggest that the attic is a symbol of concealment, of the anger repressed by women in fiction.

dream' (p. 370). Her experience as a terrorist has been relegated to the realms of the unreal, the rebellious self once more consigned to the unconscious. But this 'poor baby' is waiting to meet 'the professionals' – reality *cannot* be evaded. The narrator's choice of metaphor alerts us to the fact that the good daughter has only defeated the terrorist by retreating into a fantasy akin to infancy, by returning to the only state in which safety and security are to be found. Ironically, then, it is at this point that the repressed irrational self achieves its final victory.[2]

(iii) Narrative Technique and the Political Perspective

The splitting of Alice's psyche plays an important structural role in the novel, since it determines the duality of the plot, in which two main actions are counterpointed. Where the good daughter seeks the fulfilment of her desires and identity through the constructive act of house restoration, the terrorist seeks hers through the destruction of the existing social structure, symbolized by the bombing.

The first action, however, dominates the beginning of the novel. The detailed account of Alice's triumphs against bureaucracy, and of the practical processes involved in turning a slum into a home inevitably draws the reader vicariously into a process with which it is almost impossible not to sympathize. Such a plot conforms to the oldest of narrative patterns – the restoration of order out of chaos – satisfying an apparently widespread human need. The reader is thus interpellated into a reading position in which he or she cannot help share Alice's desires for change and improvement. The narrative method further encourages the reader to share Alice's point of view in the sense that every event is narrated from over her shoulder, as it were, in the light of its significance for her. The novel is more exclusively focused on the heroine's inner life than was *The Grass is Singing*, which allowed greater entry into other points of view. Exposed in this way to Alice's frustrations, and her anger at the inhuman waste characteristic of the consumer society, is the reader then expected to share her desires for political change, drawn inexorably along the path of anticipation which climaxes in the bombing, so that we become in a sense co-conspirators?

2. A similar process is enacted at the end of *The Yellow Wallpaper*, a short story written at the turn of the century by an American feminist, Charlotte Perkins Gilman (London: Virago, 1981).

It is tempting to reply that the reader is invited to identify only with one of Alice's selves – the conforming self that embodies the values and assumptions of the implied liberal middle-class reader. But this conforming self is, as we have seen, an unstable social construct, and moreover the frequent object of the narrator's irony. This distance between the narrator and the central character alerts us at an early stage, for instance, to Alice's blindness over Jasper, in spite of her obvious intelligence and sensitivity: when Jasper collects her dole and leaves it in her purse with a note instead of taking part of it, Alice feels gratitude that 'he did these wonderful, sweet things' (p. 103). The narrator also repeatedly reminds the reader of how much is being repressed: warnings of dissent among 'the family', which Alice does not hear, feelings of jealousy towards other couples, 'but she did not know it was that' (p. 35). The reader is thus drawn by the narrative method and the plot into identifying with a point of view which is itself ironicized and undermined. The marginal standpoint which has so often in Lessing's work provided a valuable critical perspective on the 'centre' is here itself called into question. There is no easy, comfortable position for the reader to adopt, either of detachment or of close identification with a point of view clearly presented as the authoritative one. The text instead retains that 'openness' of meaning which is such an important feature of this writer's novels.

For it is closed systems – interpretative, political, ideological – which her fiction most consistently attacks. Her earlier work suggested that even those groups on the extreme political margins adopt discursive practices which erect ideological structures in which the group itself occupies the centre ground, relegating all those who disagree to the new margins. The comrades of *The Good Terrorist* are always most united when criticizing outsiders, defining themselves in terms of what they are not. Alice justifies their exclusiveness on the grounds that 'mass parties . . . lose touch with the people' (p. 98), another unconscious irony.

This attachment to such 'closed' systems is a symptom of the extent to which, as I have already suggested, even self-styled radical parties are imbued with the inherently patriarchal values of the Western rationalist tradition. Central to those systems is the privileging of the 'rational', the intellectual and the articulate over the 'irrational', the instinctual, the practical and the non-verbal. Accordingly, while lip-service may be paid to the concept of the 'caring society', no monetary value is placed on the activity of caring in a society where money is the ultimate measure of value.[3] The doctor's theoretical knowledge of medicine is valued far more highly than the nursing care which may be essential to put theory into practice. Nor is it coincidental that the 'caring professions' have been so much associated with women, who have likewise traditionally assumed the role of 'carer' in the family. Both the practical and emotional aspects of caring have been delegated to women and in the process devalued. This is similarly true of manual labour of almost every kind, so that the distinction between manual and intellectual labour defines the barriers between classes in the most meaningful sense of that word, dividing people on the basis not simply of wealth, but of the individual's perception of his or her own relative status and value in society. Respect, authority and power accrue to those with intellectual skills.

Attachment to such systems furthermore excludes the possibility of change of a more fundamental kind, consistently evading the real problems and weaknesses of that civilization. Alice, the split subject, threatens the group's unity through her multivocal personality. When she abandons her 'meeting' voice, which adopts the discourse of the group, her personal, direct voice makes the others uncomfortable because it does not conform to the correct 'formulations'. Furthermore, while it is Alice's strong 'organ of credibility', her intuitive understanding of people and situations which so often saves the group in a crisis, enabling her to keep the police at bay and to enlist the support of bureaucrats and officials, this skill too is an object of suspicion rather than respect. And this is rightly so from the point of view of the comrades. For it enables Alice to short-cut the processes of political discourse, to *know* without being privileged to enter the meetings of those who dominate the organization. Through such means the semiotic of body language, of currents or waves of feeling, undermines the symbolic order.

By returning so specifically to the split subject as the site of conflicting ideologies, Doris Lessing demonstrates a continuing belief in the crucial importance of ideological processes in determining individual motivation and social organization. Moreover, by exploring that subject within the context of contemporary British society, she confronts head on questions of politics, choice and commitment which earlier novels might seem to evade. Specifically, she seems to me to indicate the failure of existing political parties to pursue truly radical paths, to engage critically with the validity of their own assumptions

3. Lessing's earlier novel, *The Diary of a Good Neighbour* (1983), first published under the pseudonym of Jane Somers, is a powerful condemnation of society's failure either to 'care' adequately or to value those that do the caring.

and most deeply held beliefs. Alice tries to be both 'the good daughter' following essentially liberal, humanist traditions by looking for practical, reasonable solutions to the problems of individuals, and the 'terrorist', committed to the total restructuring of society in the interests of a whole class, but she cannot be both, since the discourse of patriarchal humanism and revolutionary Marxism meet in violent conflict. The novel suggests the need to cut across categories, to avoid pigeonholes and all closed systems which demand either/or simplifications. What is implicitly offered is the kind of radical feminist perspective which does not seek to substitute one set of power relations for another, but to find totally different patterns of relationship. This is the only consistently 'marginal' perspective, since it does not automatically claim the centre ground for itself, but offers instead a radically different way of seeing – non-categorical and non-hierarchical.

In Place of a Conclusion

When I planned this book, I intended in my Conclusion to attempt a summing up of Doris Lessing's literary career. The links between her first and latest novel led me to anticipate drawing some kind of circle around her novels, as the title of the previous chapter perhaps indicates. In the process of writing, however, I became increasingly aware that to attempt such a summary or to attempt to delimit the significance of her work would be in complete contradiction of what her novels themselves demand of the reader – an awareness of their multivalence, of their openness to interpretation of many kinds.

To underline this point, since then Lessing has published another novel, *The Fifth Child*, which represents yet another departure. Incorporating folklore elements in the idea of a changeling child, and arising out of the novelist's speculations about the effect of a misplaced gene, of a race being born out of time and place, it has been called a 'horror story' by some critics. The novel is concerned with the nature of evil, and the ability of the individual, and society as a whole, to cope with it, taking still further this writer's exploration of the most challenging issues facing the contemporary world.

Suggesting as it does the inadequacy of 'civilized' values to cope with such phenomena, Lessing's latest novel appears deeply pessimistic, but the author herself remains optimistic about our long-term future in so far as she believes individuals and societies are developing a greater ability than ever before to distance themselves from their behaviour and criticize it. And it is this element of distance that the marginal perspective which is the most consistent feature of her fiction fosters and provides an analytical base for. There are possibly dangers in such a perspective: it could be said that it condemns the observer to disengagement from the centre and a resultant loss of power, even while it preserves the integrity of the observer. Cynics may accuse such an observer of being 'out of touch' with the realities of the centre. Lessing's answer could, I believe, be summed up in the words of Joanna Russ:

> Only on the margins does growth occur.
> (*How to Suppress Women's Writing*, Women's Press, 1984)

Select Bibliography

Place of publication is in all cases London, except where otherwise stated.

Students of Doris Lessing's fiction will find her non-fiction interesting and enlightening. *Going Home* (Michael Joseph, 1957) provides an account of her return visit to Southern Africa, while *In Pursuit of the English: A Documentary* (MacGibbon & Kee, 1960) presents her impressions of England and the English. *A Small Personal Voice: Essays, Reviews, Interviews* ed. Paul Schlueter (New York: Alfred A. Knopf, 1974) is an extremely useful collection of her views on politics and literature.

A number of short, general introductions to Lessing's fiction is now readily available, the most accessible probably being Lorna Sage, *Doris Lessing*, Contemporary Writers Series (Methuen, 1983). This provides a succinct and authoritative survey of Lessing's themes and methods, but for more detailed analysis of individual texts, you will need to consult one of the larger-scale studies. Paul Schlueter, *The Novels of Doris Lessing* (Carbondale and Edwardsville, Southern Illinois University Press, 1973) provides a more developed survey of the novels which is sound, if rather basic, and of course does not cover the later fiction. More up-to-date is Mona Knapp, *Doris Lessing* (Literature and Life Series, New York: Ungar Publishing Company, 1984), which provides a very helpful biography as well as an intelligent survey of all Lessing's work, including the *Canopus* sequence.

Of the more specialized studies, Michael Thorpe, *Doris Lessing's Africa* (Evans Brothers, 1978) relates the author's African novels to their context and provides a useful Bibliography for that background. Students already familiar with Lessing's fiction and with the mainstream critical approaches should try Roberta Rubenstein, *The*

Novelistic Vision of Doris Lessing: Breaking the Forms of Consciousness, (Urbana and Chicago, Ill.: University of Illinois Press, 1979), which provides an interesting Jungian approach to Lessing's fiction.

Some of the most interesting criticism is, however, to be found in collections which bring together a variety of different critical approaches and cover a variety of texts. The best of these are *Doris Lessing: Critical Studies* ed. Annis Pratt and L.S. Dembo (Madison, Wisc.: University of Wisconsin Press, 1974), which also contains interesting interviews with Lessing, and *Notebooks/Memoirs/Archives: Reading and Rereading Doris Lessing* ed. Jenny Taylor (Routledge & Kegan Paul, 1982). Taylor's Introduction to this volume provides an excellent analysis of the context – intellectual, political and literary – of Lessing's work, and the book also includes a useful bibliography of articles about it. A more recent collection edited by Harold Bloom – *Doris Lessing* (Modern Critical Views, New York: Chelsea House Publishers, 1986) – contains extracts from the studies by Sage, Schlueter and Rubenstein, as well as a useful review of *The Good Terrorist* by Alison Lurie.

For consideration of the feminist influence on Lessing, read the relevant chapters in Sydney Janet Kaplan, *Feminist Consciousness in the Modern British Novel* (Champaign: University of Illinois Press, 1975), and Elaine Showalter, *A Literature of Their Own: British Women Novelists from Bronte to Lessing* (Virago, 1978). For more information about Sufism and its influence, read Nancy S. Hardin, 'The Sufi Teaching Story and Doris Lessing', *Twentieth Century Literature* 23 (1977), pp. 314–26, and 'Doris Lessing and the Sufi Way' in Pratt and Dembo, *Critical Studies*, pp. 148–64. Lessing's own comments on Sufism can be found in 'In the World, Not of It', in Taylor, *Notebooks*, pp. 129–38.

For a fuller bibliography of Lessing's writing and criticism of her work, consult Selma R. Burkom, *Doris Lessing: A Checklist of Primary and Secondary Sources* (New York: Whitson Publishing, 1973), or for a more up-to-date listing of secondary material, Dee Seligman, *Doris Lessing: An Annotated Bibliography of Criticism* (Westport: Greenwood Press, 1980).

Chronological Table

1919   Doris Cook born in Persia (now Iran) of British parents

1924   Moved with her family to a farm in Southern Rhodesia (now Zimbabwe). Attended convent school in Salisbury (now Harare) till aged 14, but largely self-taught through reading literary classics ordered from England.

1934   Moved into Salisbury to work as a nursemaid.

1936   Returned to farm, wrote and destroyed several 'bad' novels.

1938   Returned to Salisbury to work as a telephonist, and became politicized because of views on colour bar; joined left-wing group which eventually formed the basis of the Communist party.

1939   Married Frank Wisdom, had a son and daughter; feeling increasingly alienated from colonial society.

1943   Divorced. Meeting regularly with RAF men serving in the colony on a war-time basis, Socialists and Communists, many of them refugees from Nazi Germany.

1945   Married Gottfried Lessing, one of those refugees; worked as typist first in legal offices, then for Hansard.

1947   Had a son, Peter; left job to write *The Grass is Singing* and first African short stories.

1949   Divorced, and moved with her son to London, where she worked as a shorthand typist before the success of her novel enabled her to make a living as a professional writer.

1950   *The Grass is Singing* published in London by Michael Joseph, who remained her main publisher until 1965, and in New York by T.Y. Crowell. The novel was reprinted seven times within five months.

1951   *This was the Old Chief's Country* (short stories) published,

Lessing regarded as a powerful new talent, in spite of some grumblings from right-wing critics about her preoccupation with racial questions.

1952   *Martha Quest*
L. visited Russia as member of Communist Party.

1953   *Five: Short Novels*; received Somerset Maugham Memorial Prize the following year.

1954   *A Proper Marriage*

1956   Revisited Southern Rhodesia, in spite of being declared a prohibited immigrant because of her views on the colour bar, but was barred from entering South Africa. L. left Communist Party over its defence of Soviet invasion of Hungary, and after revelations of effects of Stalinist policy made at Twentieth Party Congress.

1957   Published account of this visit in *Going Home*. Contributed 'The Small Personal Voice' to *Declaration*, a collection of essays by leading young writers on the role of the radical intelligentsia, edited by Tom Maschler.

1958   Involved in organizing first CND march from Aldermaston.
Each his own Wilderness (play) performed at the Royal Court, London.
A Ripple from the Storm
In the late 1950s, L. underwent Jungian psychotherapy, and had experience of other people's mental breakdowns, both of which she drew on for the novels written in the 60s and 70s. She later came to feel that Jung was limited in comparison to the Eastern philosophy from which she felt his ideas derived.

1960   *In Pursuit of the English* (documentary) published. L now established, on the basis of her African writing, as an important committed realist of radical views.

1962   *The Golden Notebook*'s publication therefore met with mixed reactions, some reviews finding it muddled, while others saw it as confirming her position as our 'best woman novelist' and one of the best writers of the post-war generation (*Sunday Times*).

1963   *A Man and Two Women* (short stories)

1964   *African Stories*
Martha Quest and *A Proper Marriage* reissued as Vols. I and II of *Children of Violence* series by McGibbon & Kee, who bought the publishing rights for the series from Michael Joseph. Reviewed Idries Shah, *The Sufis* enthusiastically in 'An Elephant in the Dark'. Continued to read and review Shah's books published in the 60s and 70s, and to be greatly influenced by Sufi philosophy.

1965   *Landlocked* (Vol. IV)

1966   *A Ripple from the Storm* (Vol. V)

During the late 60s, L. further developed her interest in psycho-analysis and the paranormal, reading a great deal of science fiction, including writers as various as Isaac Asimov and Eric Von Daniken. These influences together with that of Sufism are evident in much of her later fiction, first and notably in the final volume of the *Children of Violence* sequence published in

1969   *The Four-Gated City.*
Visited State University of New York at Stony Brook at a time of considerable campus unrest. An interview recorded there (later published in *A Small Personal Voice* 1975) discusses her loss of a certain kind of political belief and the problems facing the New Left. It also demonstrates her familiarity with both Freudian and Jungian psychology.

1971   *Briefing for a Descent into Hell* published by Jonathan Cape, who became her main publisher.

1975   *Memoirs of a Survivor* published, made into a film in 1981.
In the late 70s L read the sacred books of the Old and New Testament, the Apocrypha and the Koran, finding common links to be used in the *Canopus in Argos* sequence, the first volume of which was published in

1979   *Shikasta*

1980   *The Marriages between Zones Three, Four and Five* (Vol. II)

1981   *The Sirian Experiments* (Vol. III)

1982   *The Making of the Representative for Planet 8* (Vol. IV)

1983   *The Sentimental Agents in the Volyen Empire* (Vol. V)
This sequence won L. a new kind of readership, although it also lost many of her earlier fans.
L. also published *The Diary of a Good Neighbour* under the pseudonym of Jane Somers, in order to be judged and reviewed on merit. Cape rejected the manuscript, but Michael Joseph, her first publisher, accepted it. Reviewers generally treated it rather patronizingly, with a few exceptions.

1985   *The Good Terrorist* published, nominated for Booker prize, won W.H. Smith award.

1988   *The Fifth Child* published.

Index